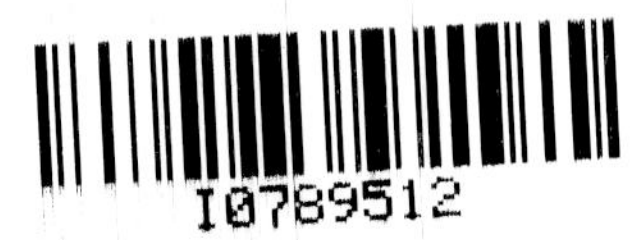

Beautiful dove images design paperback

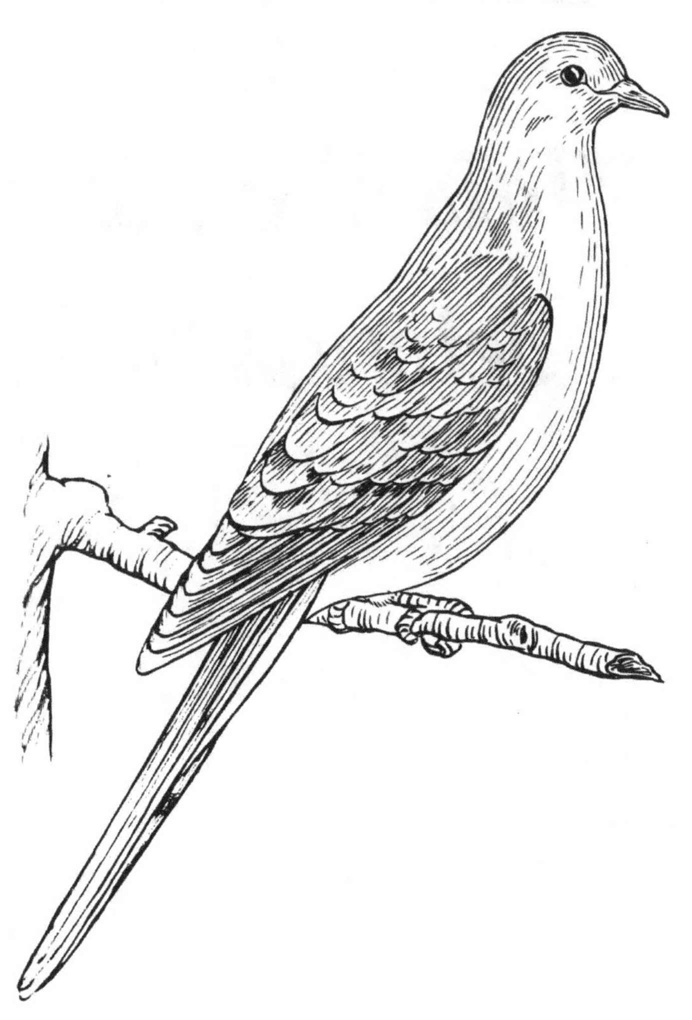

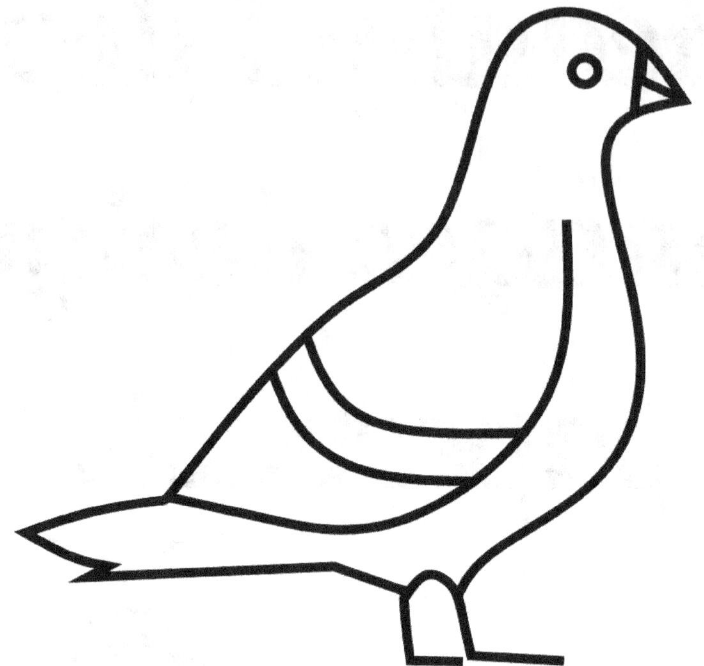

This book is
belongs to

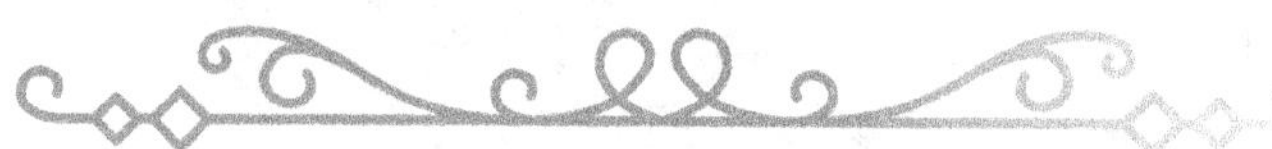

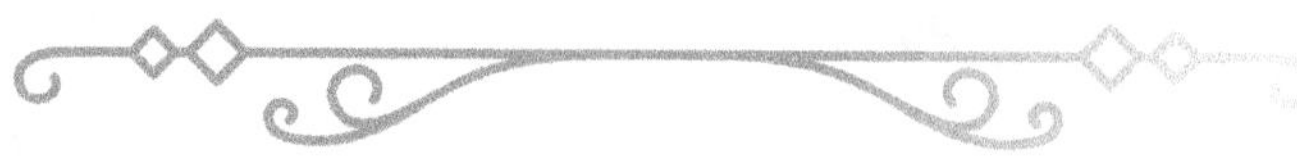

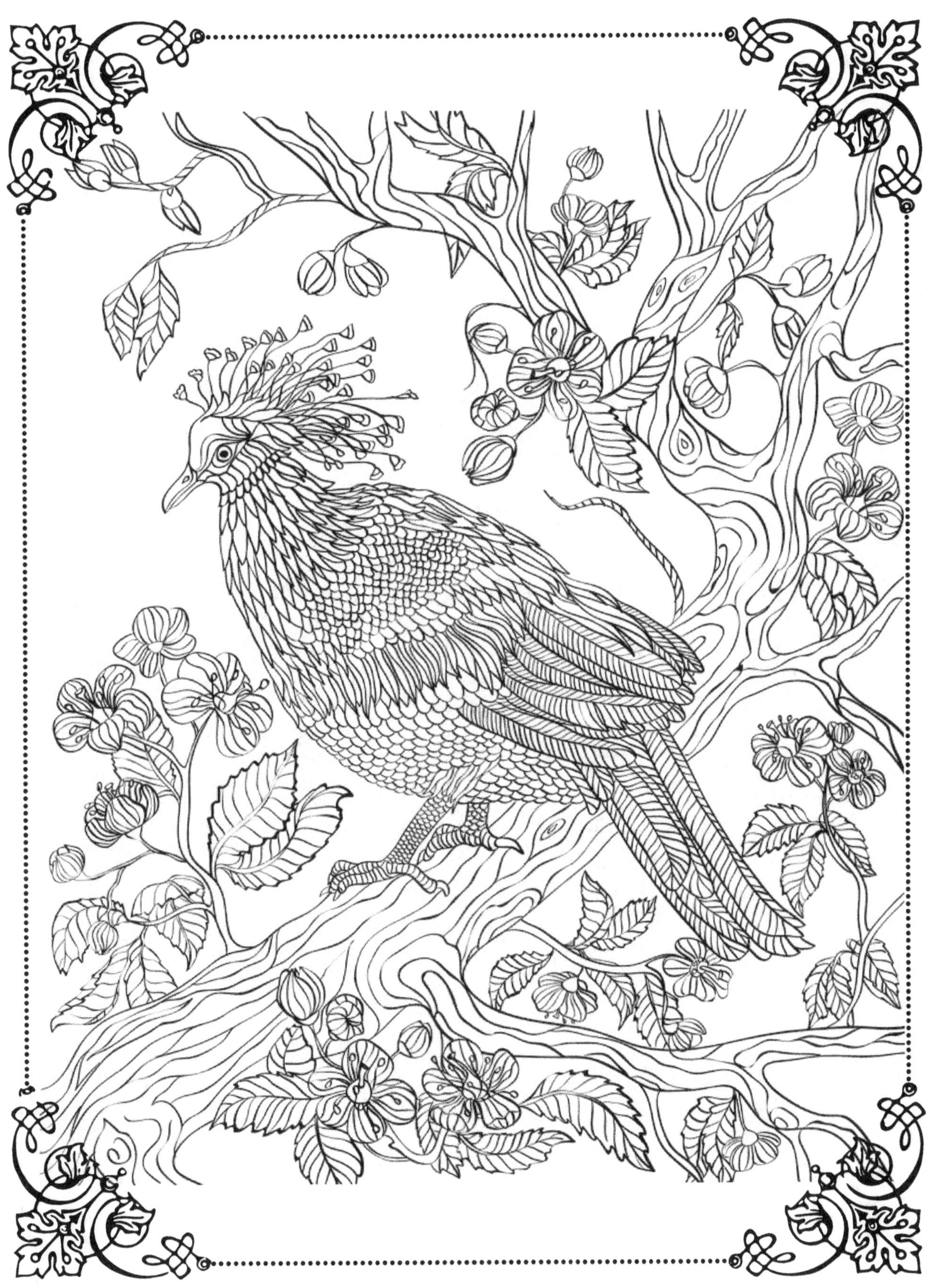

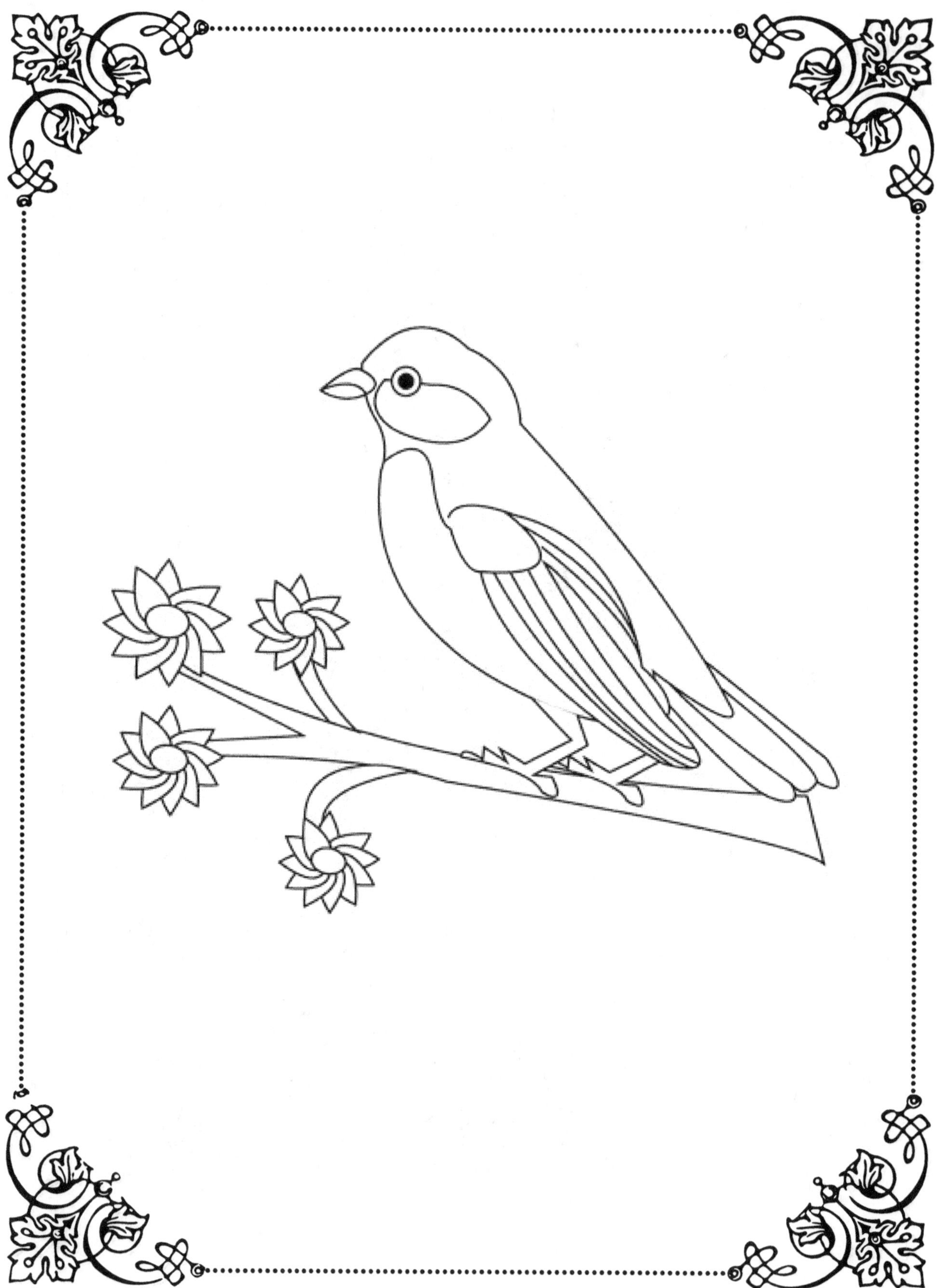

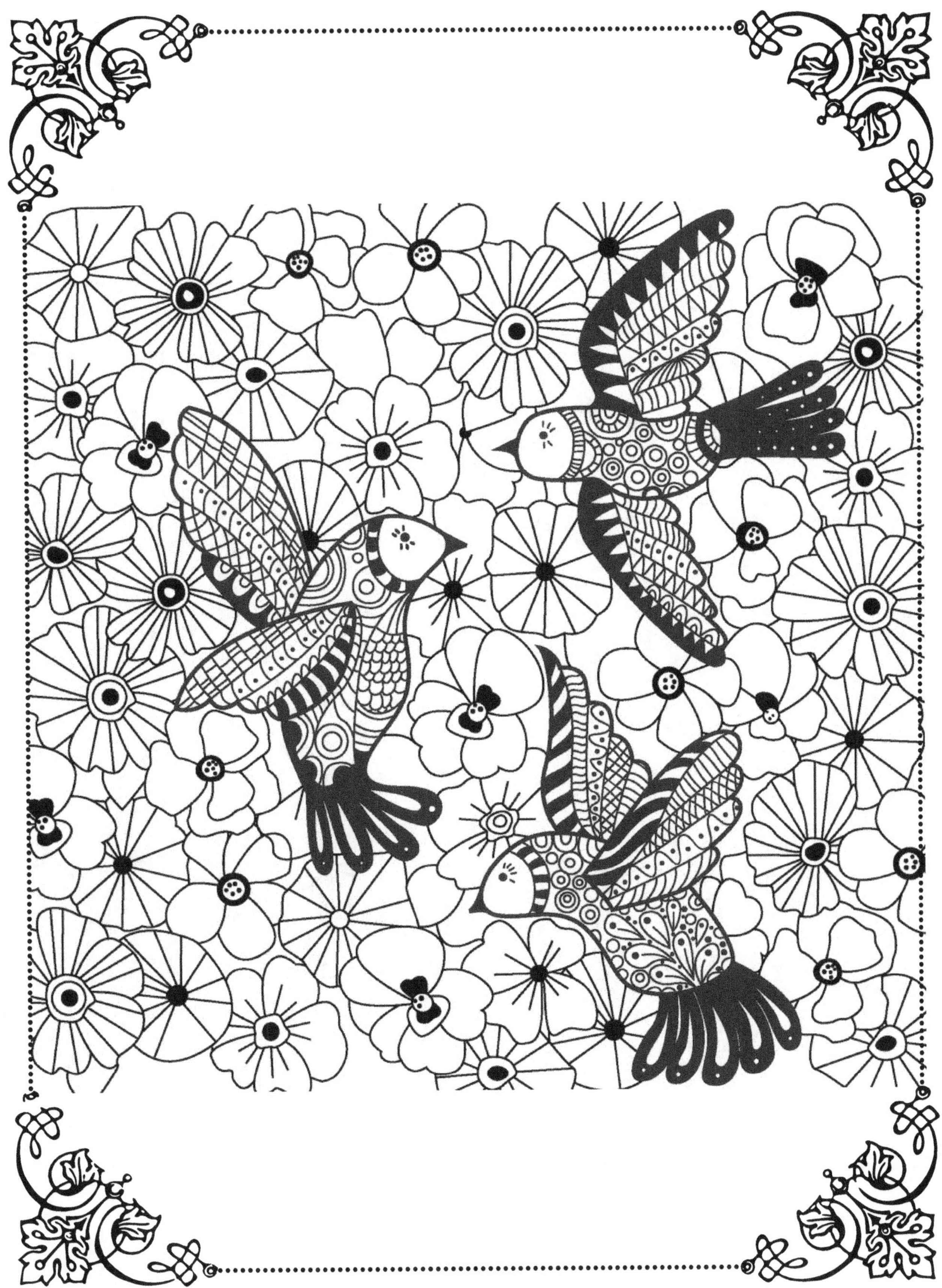

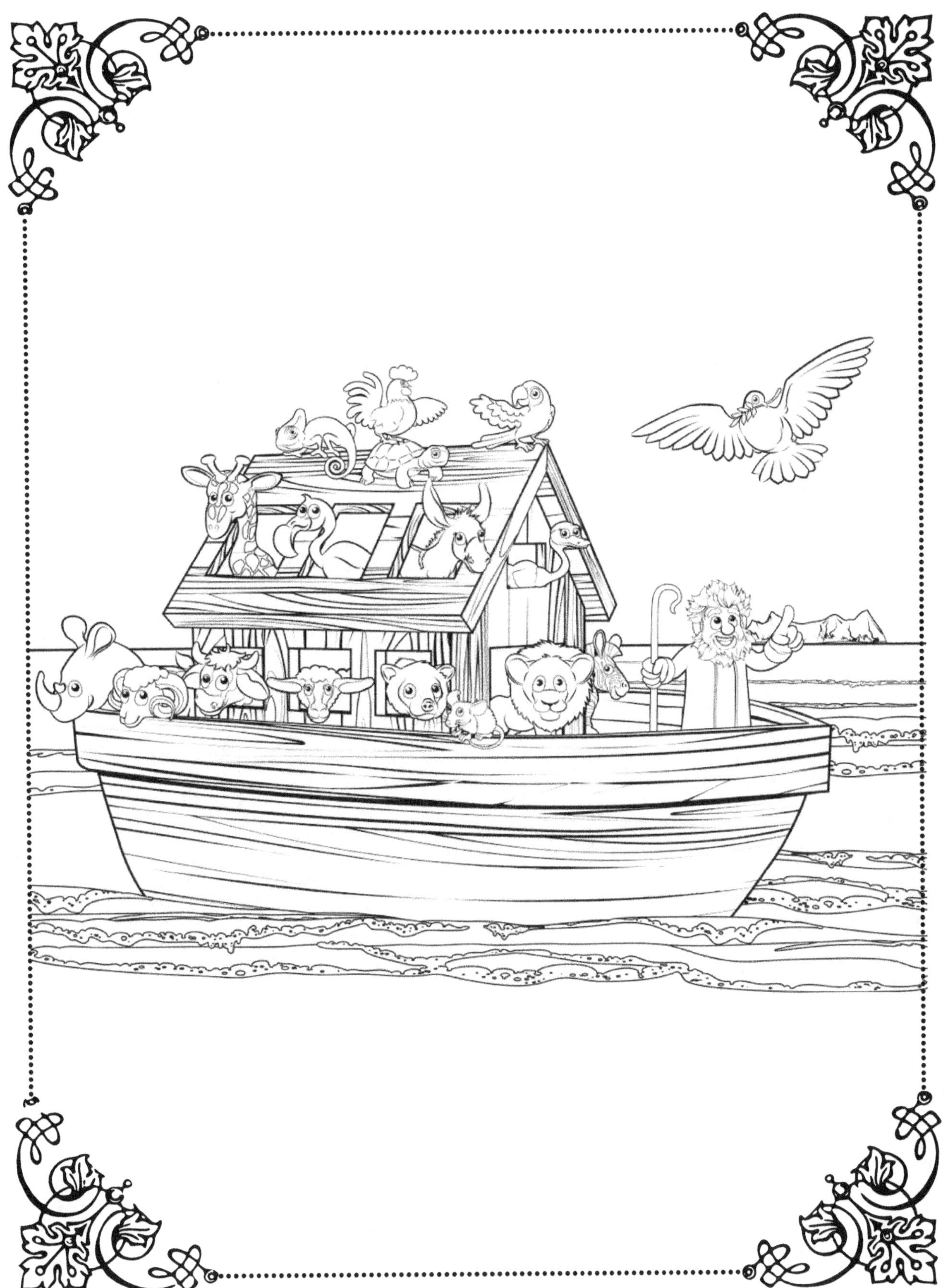

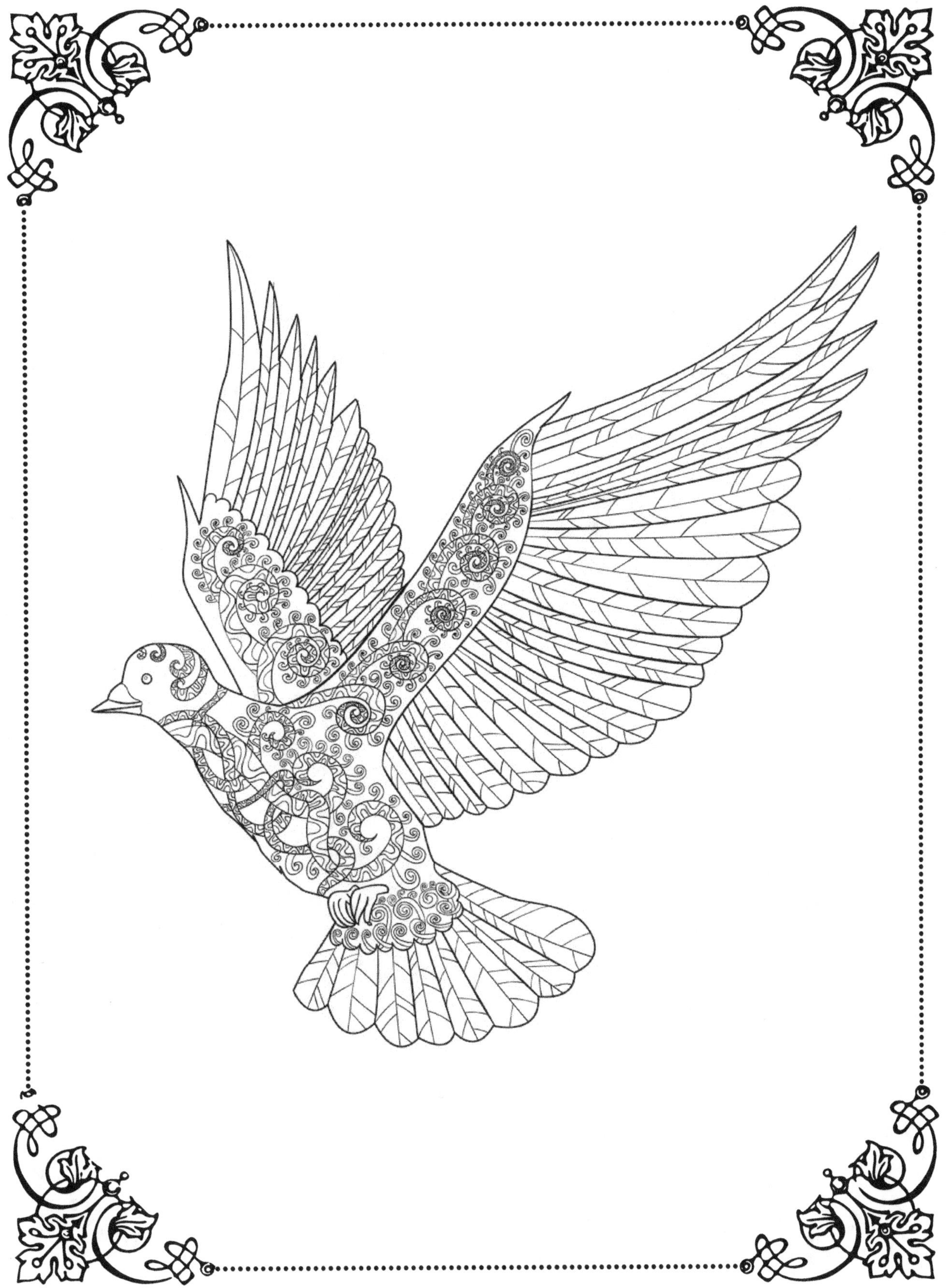

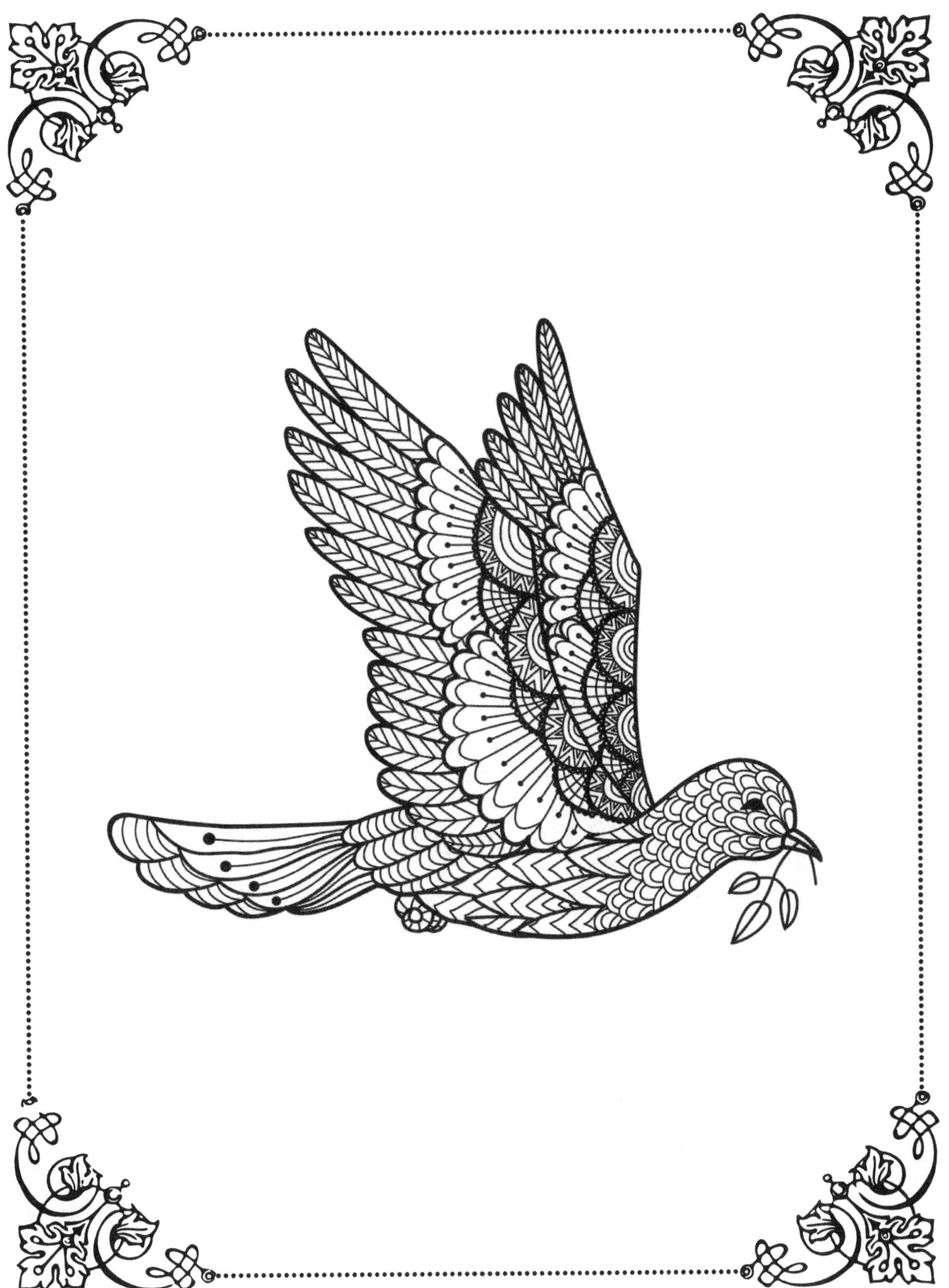

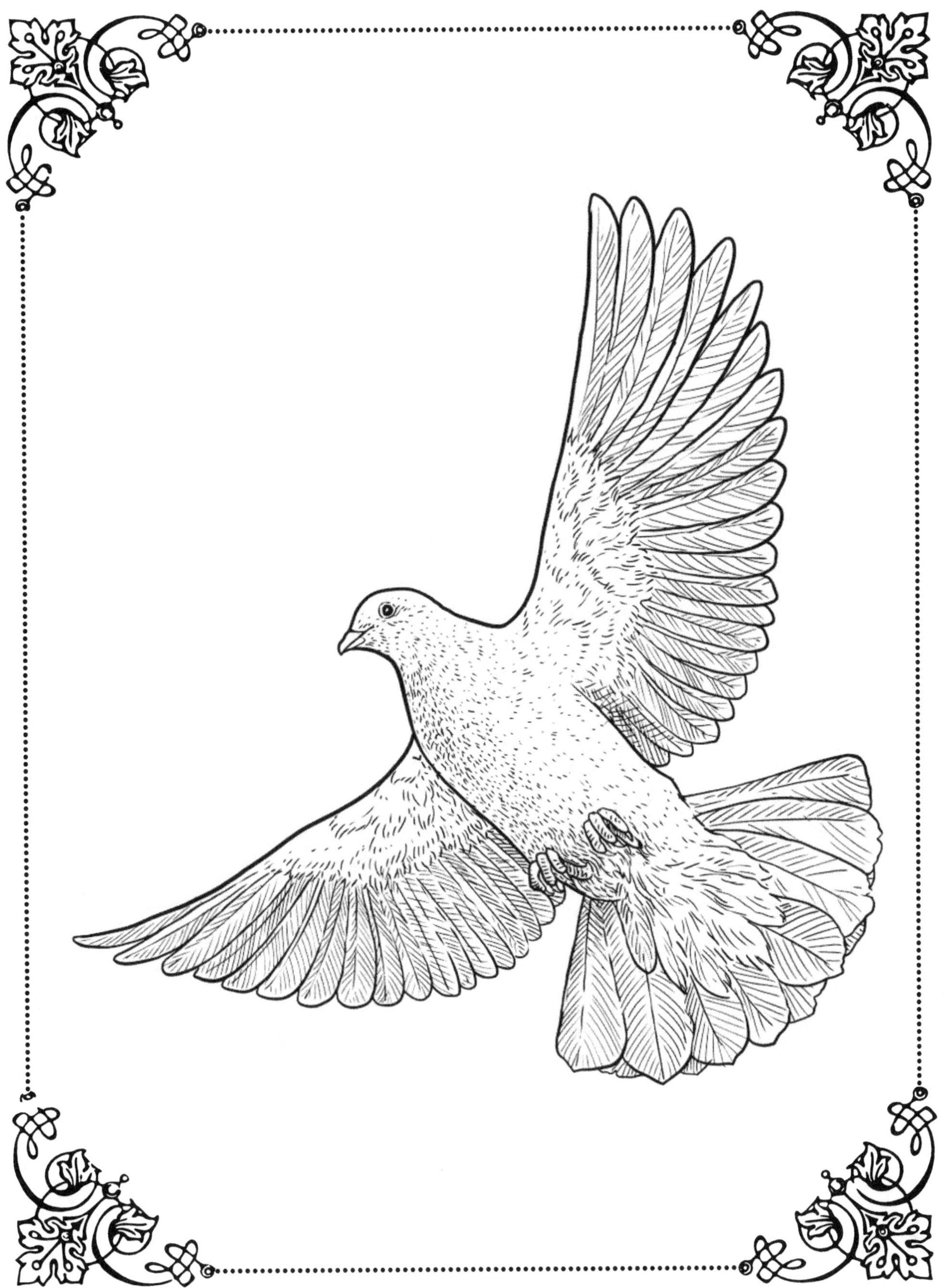

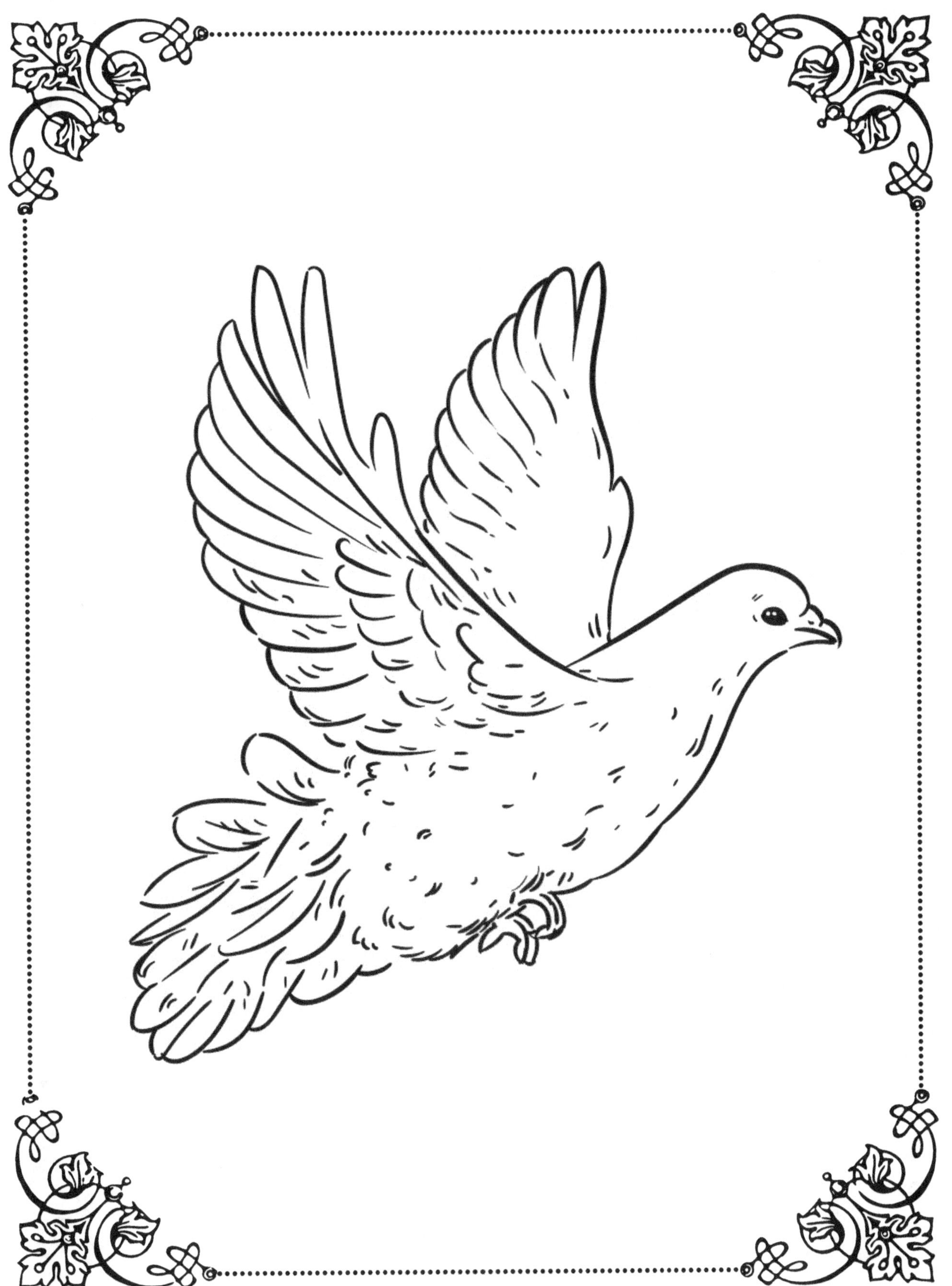

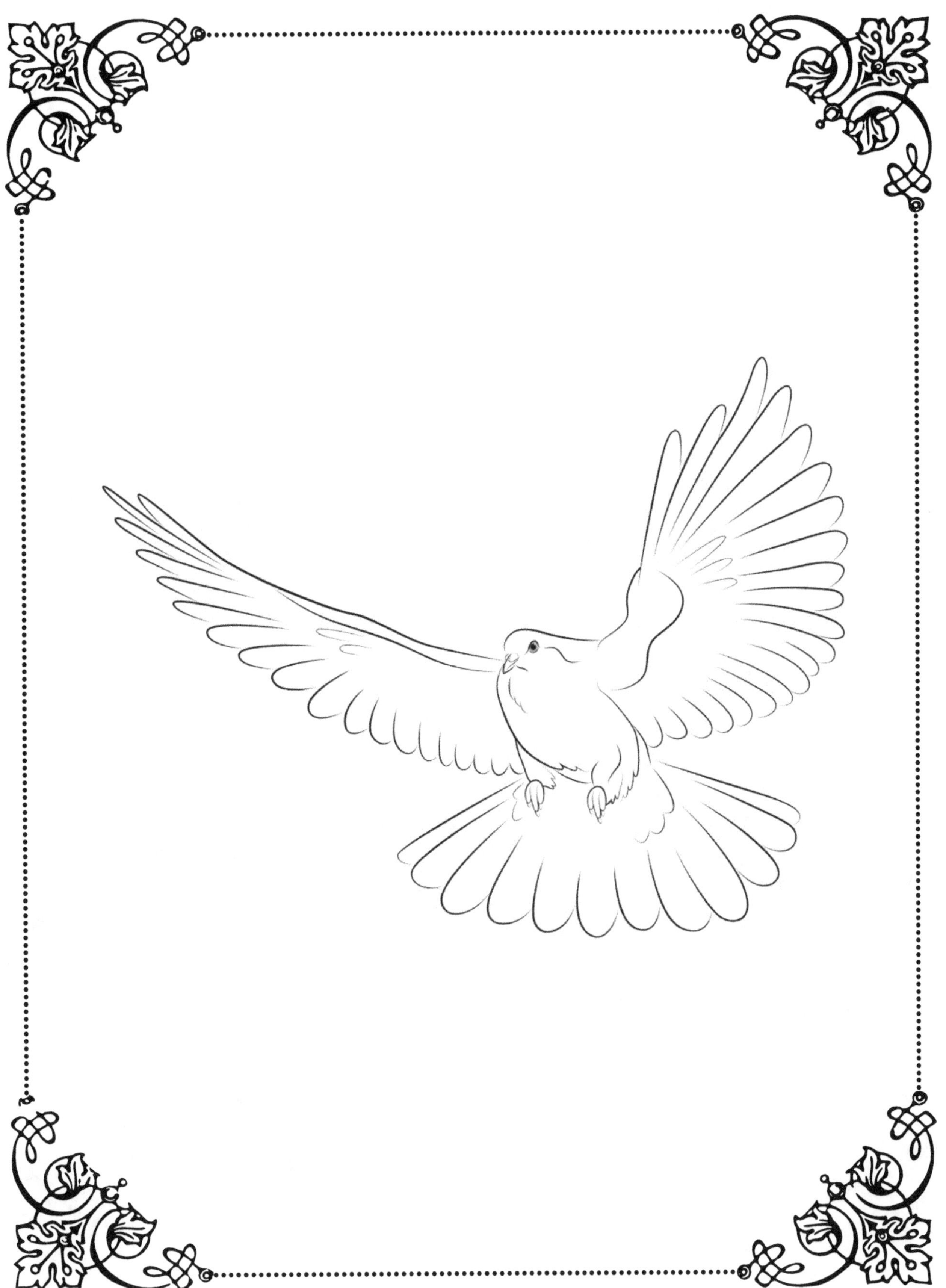

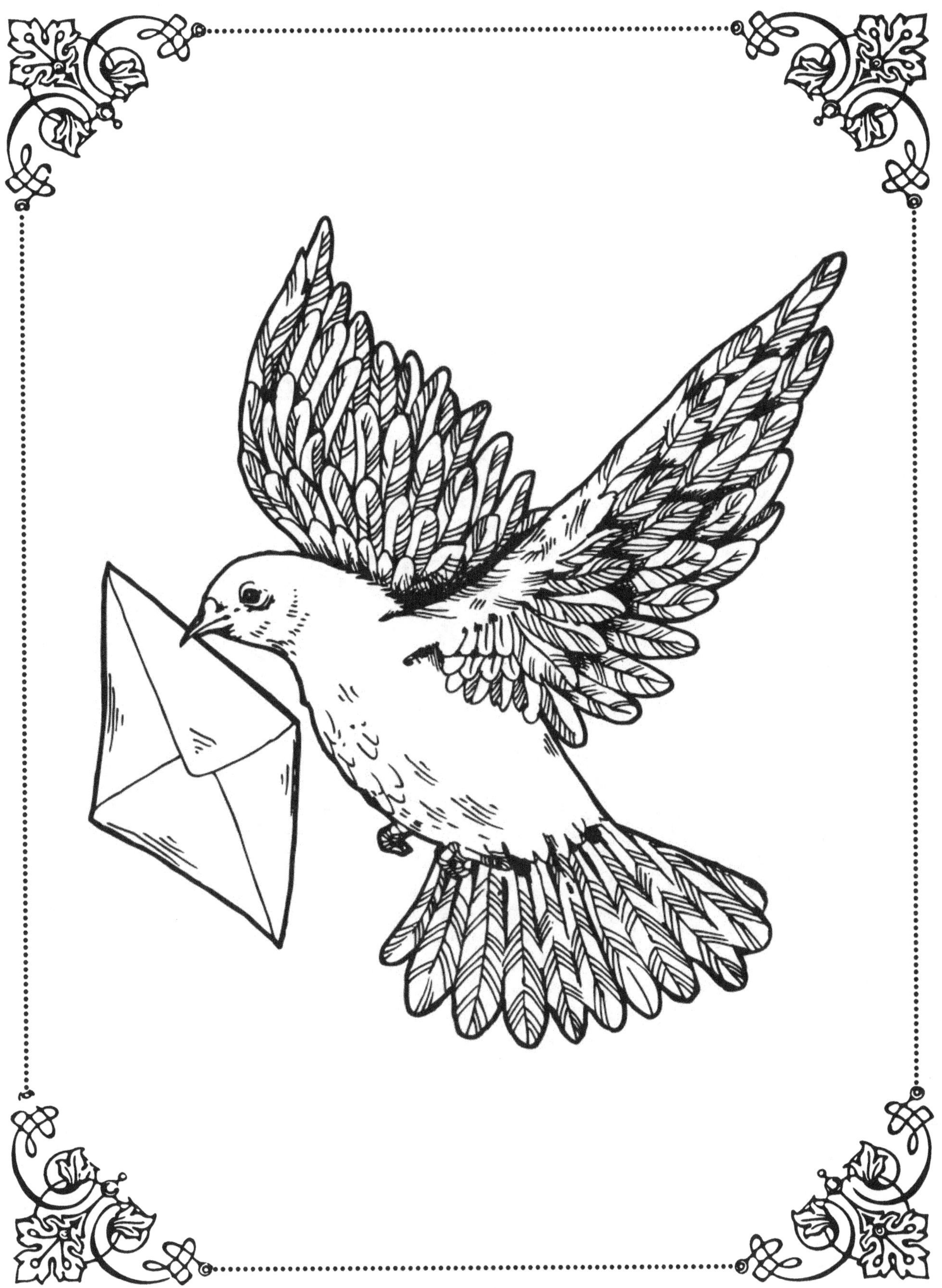

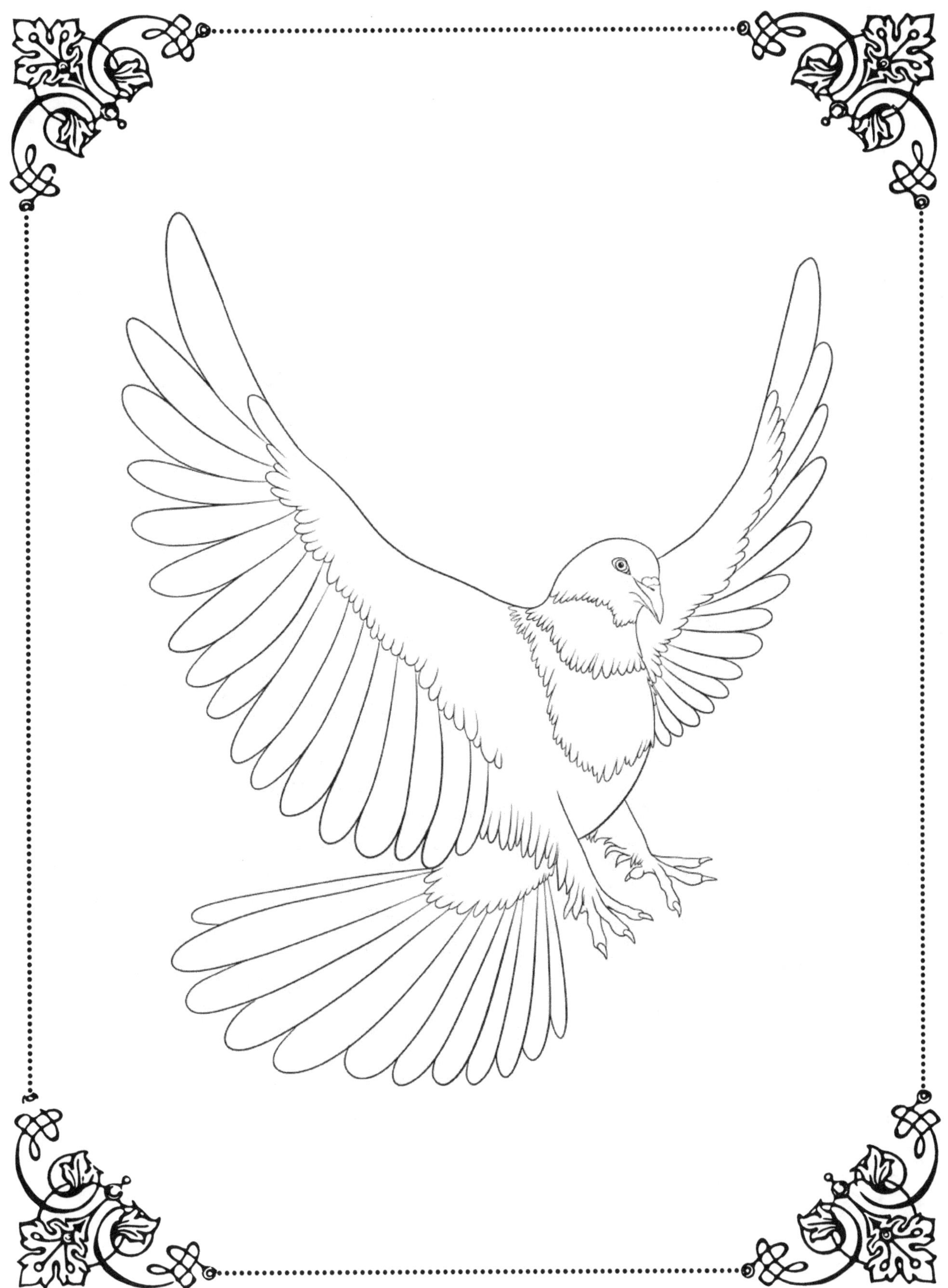

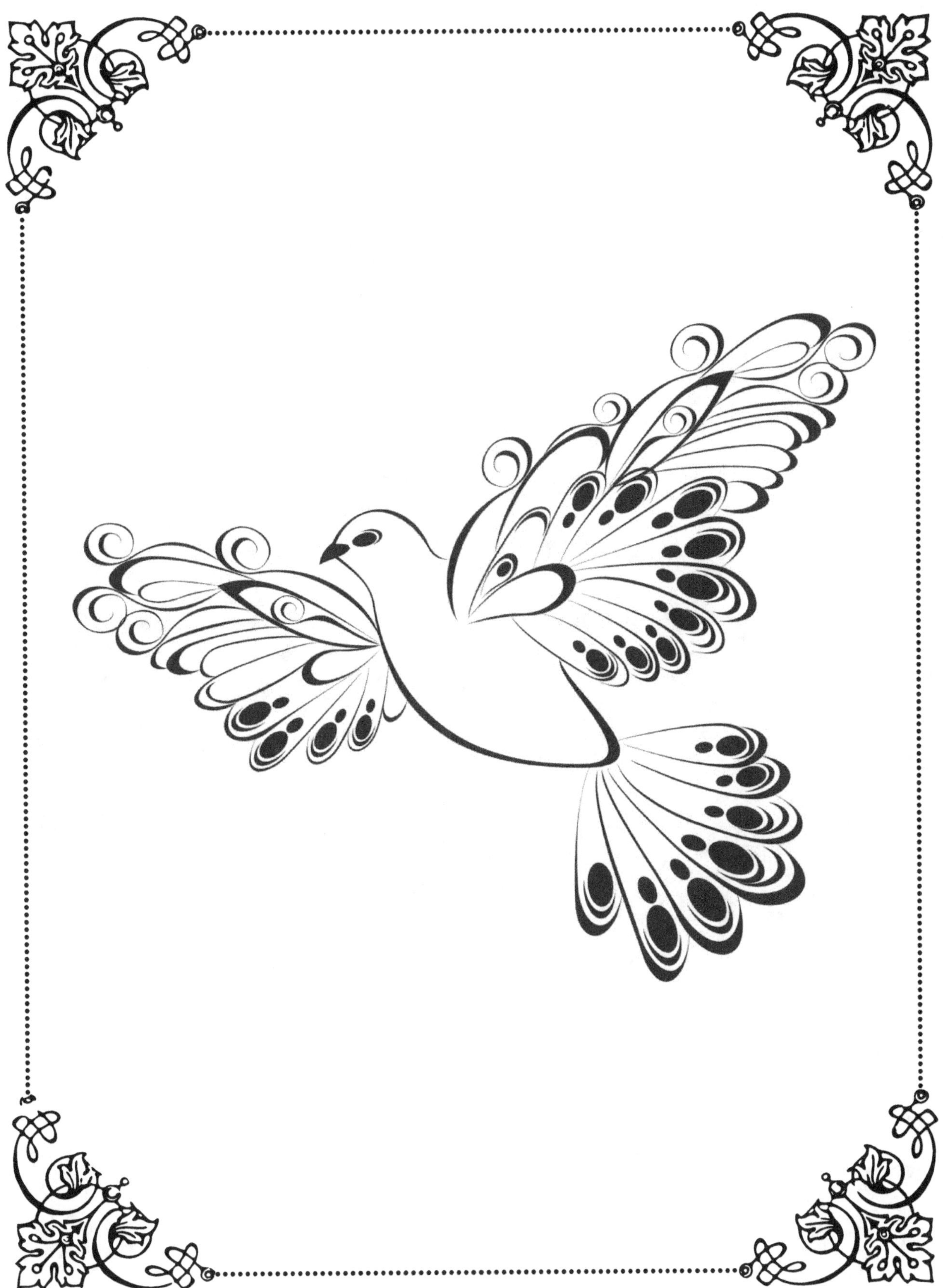

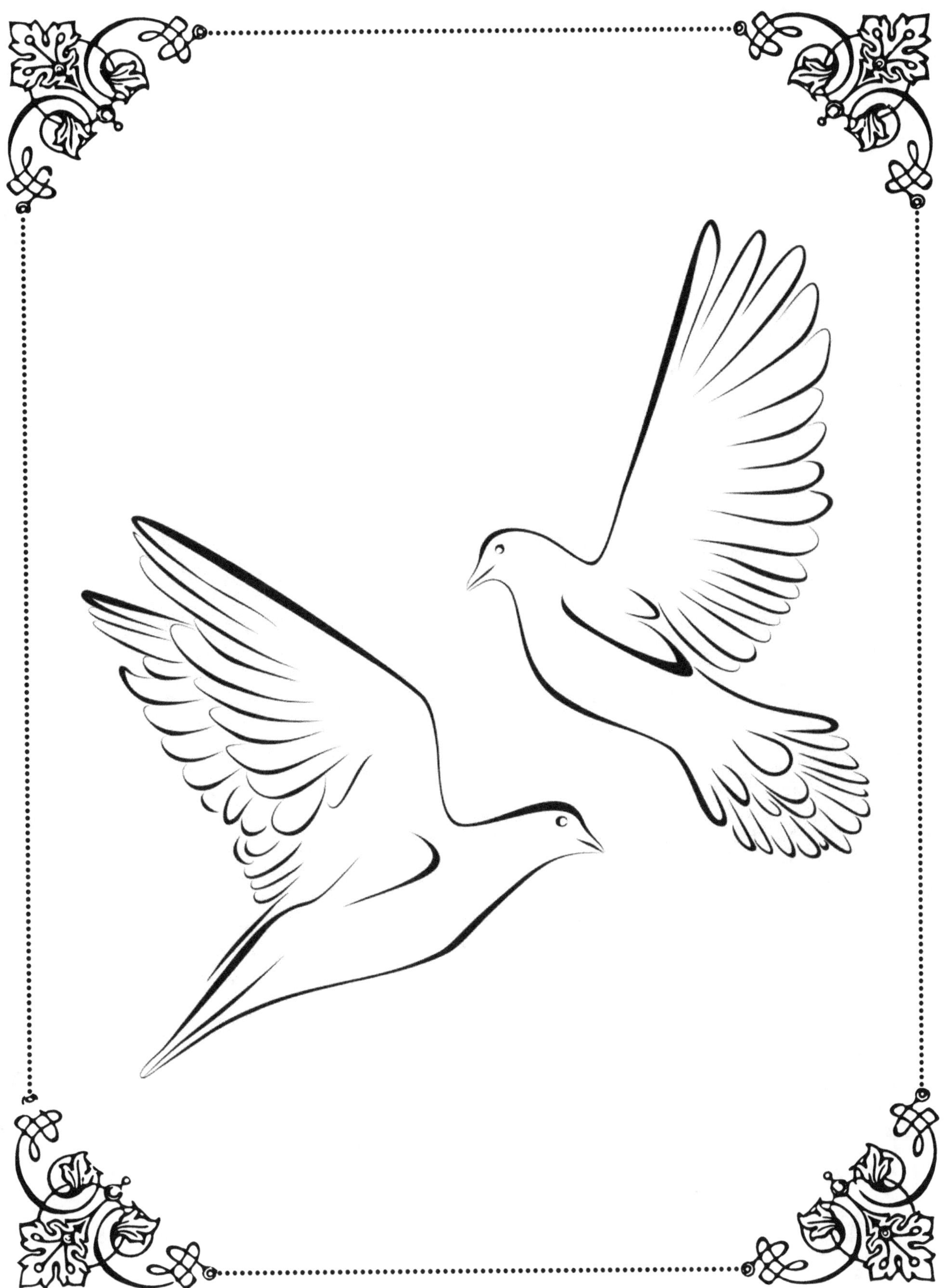

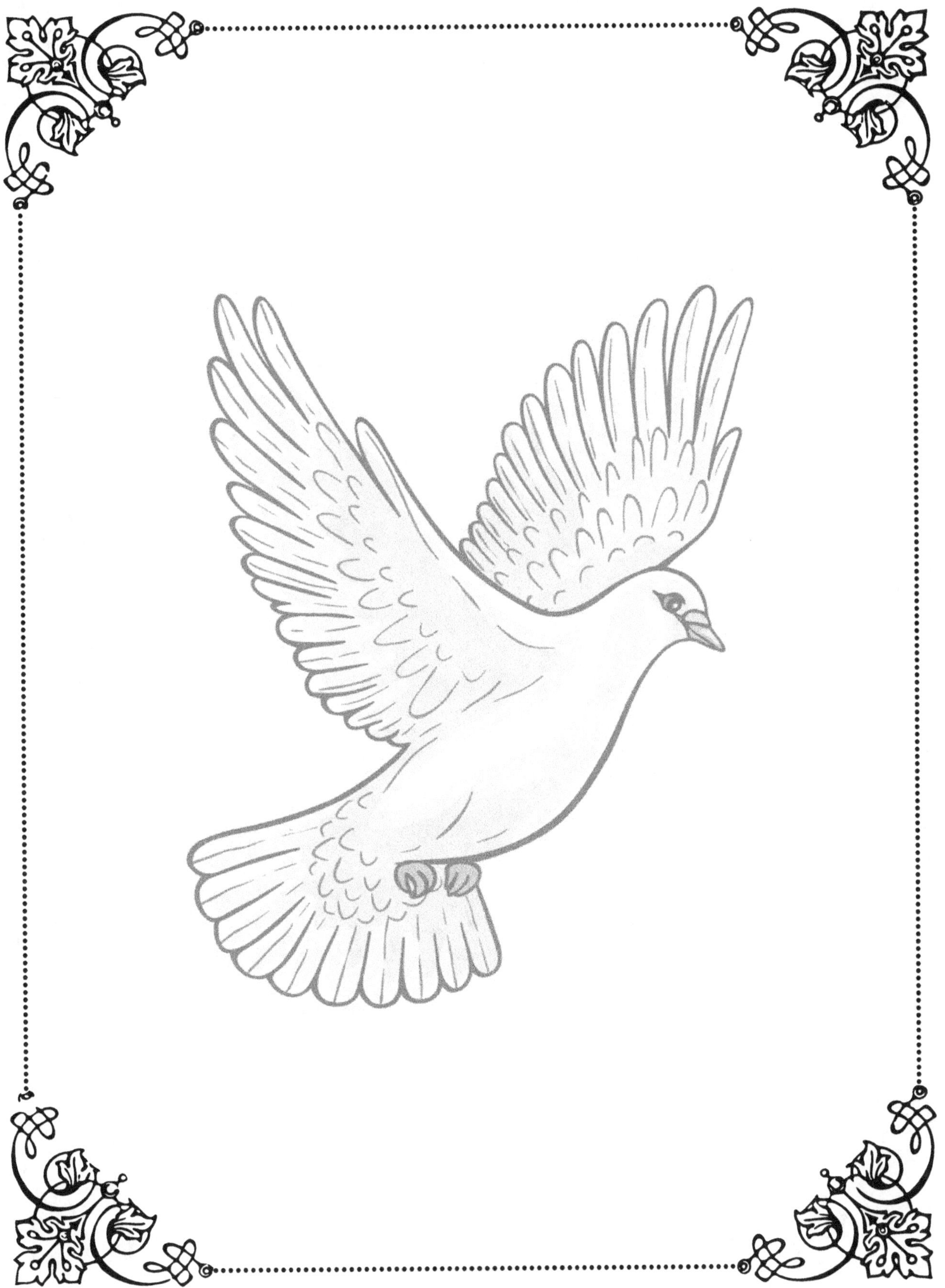

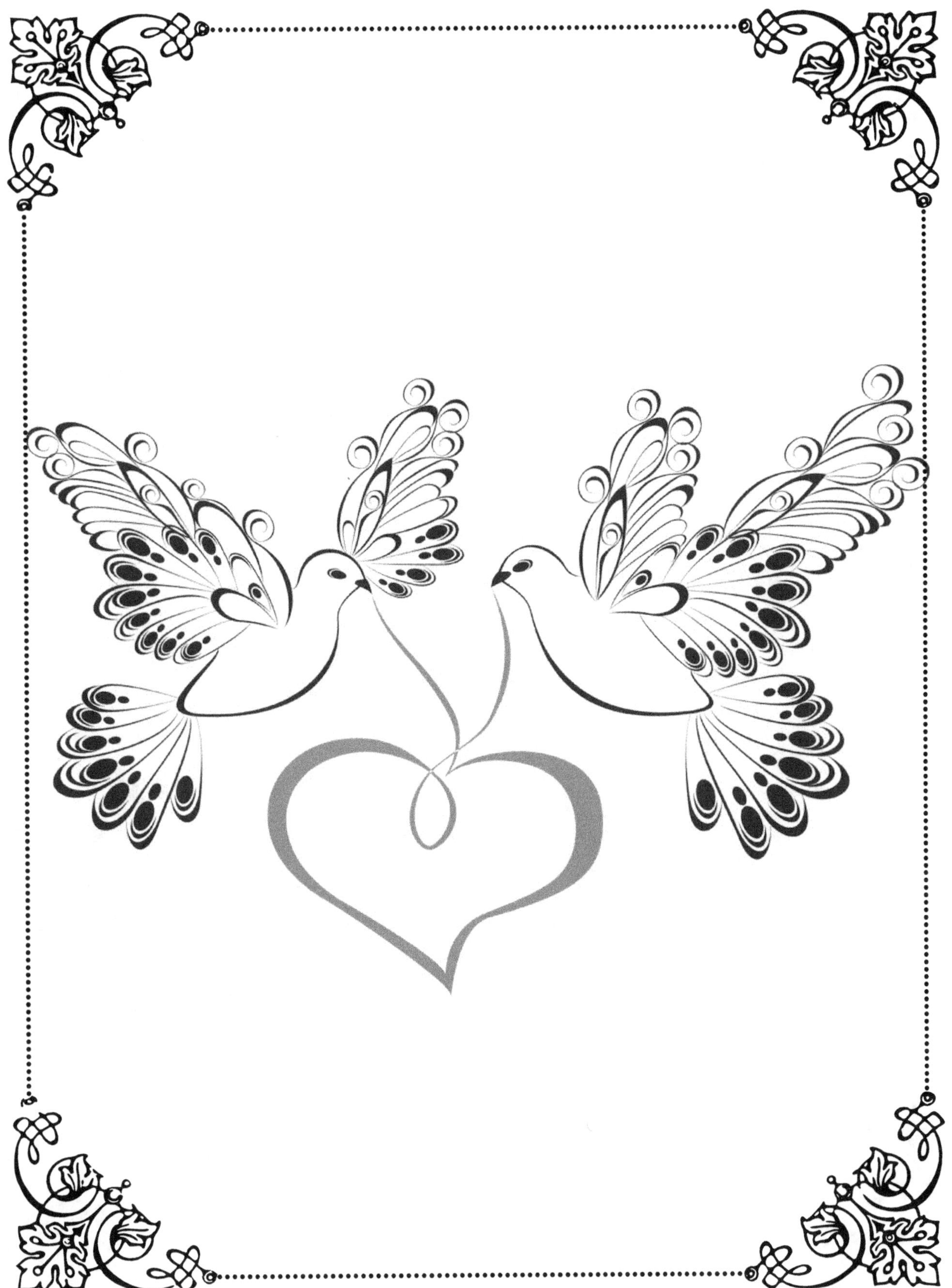

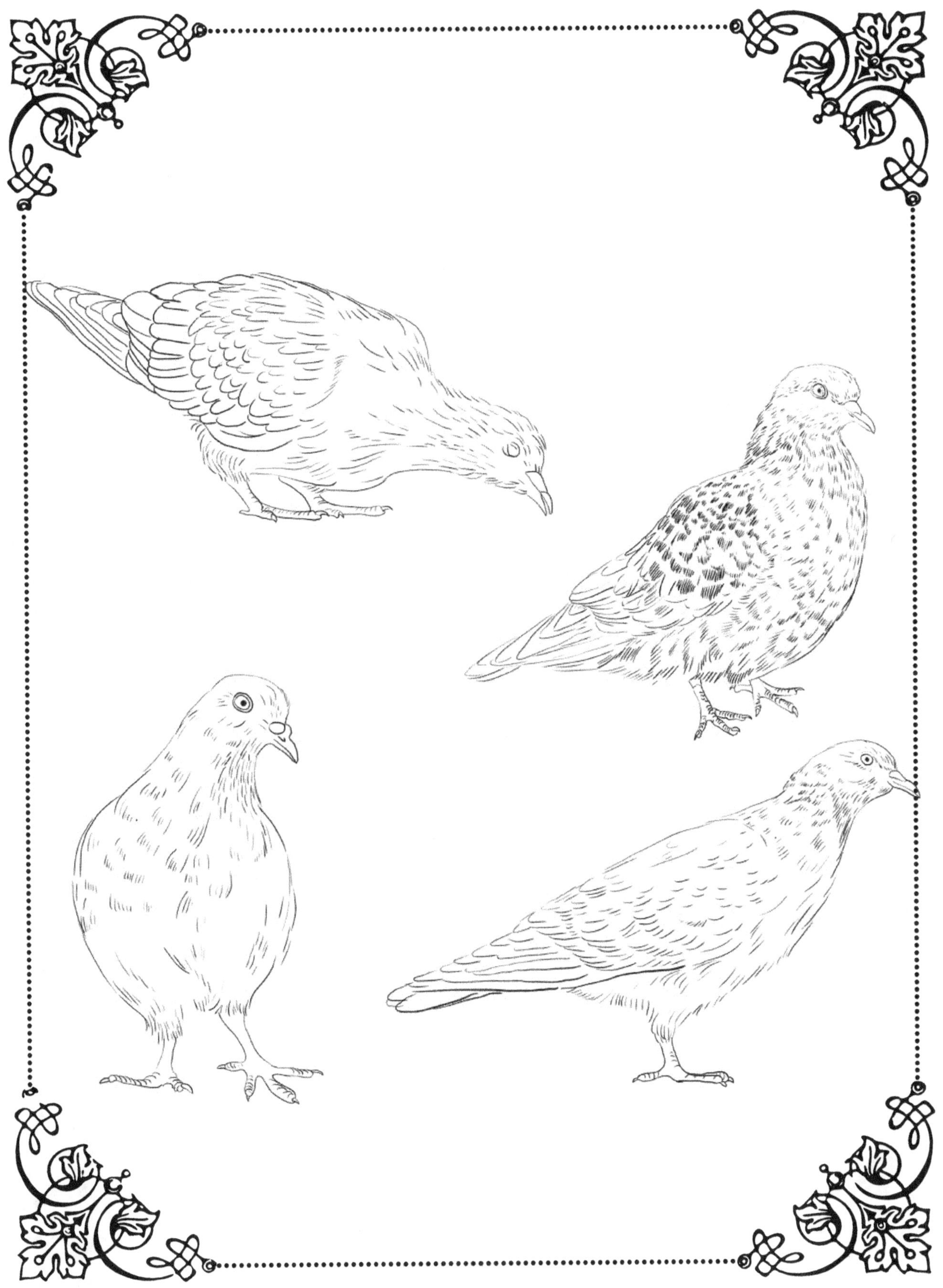

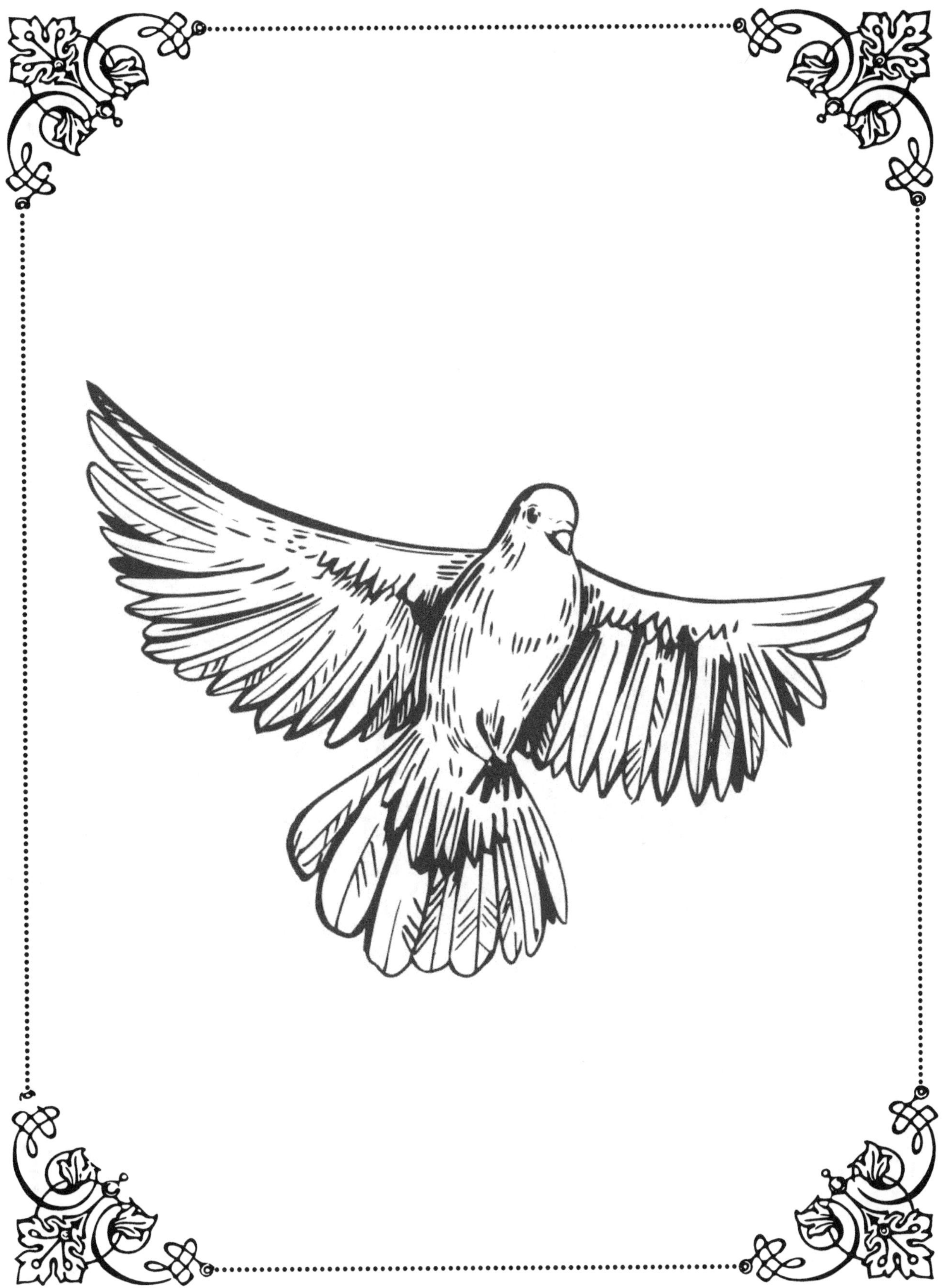

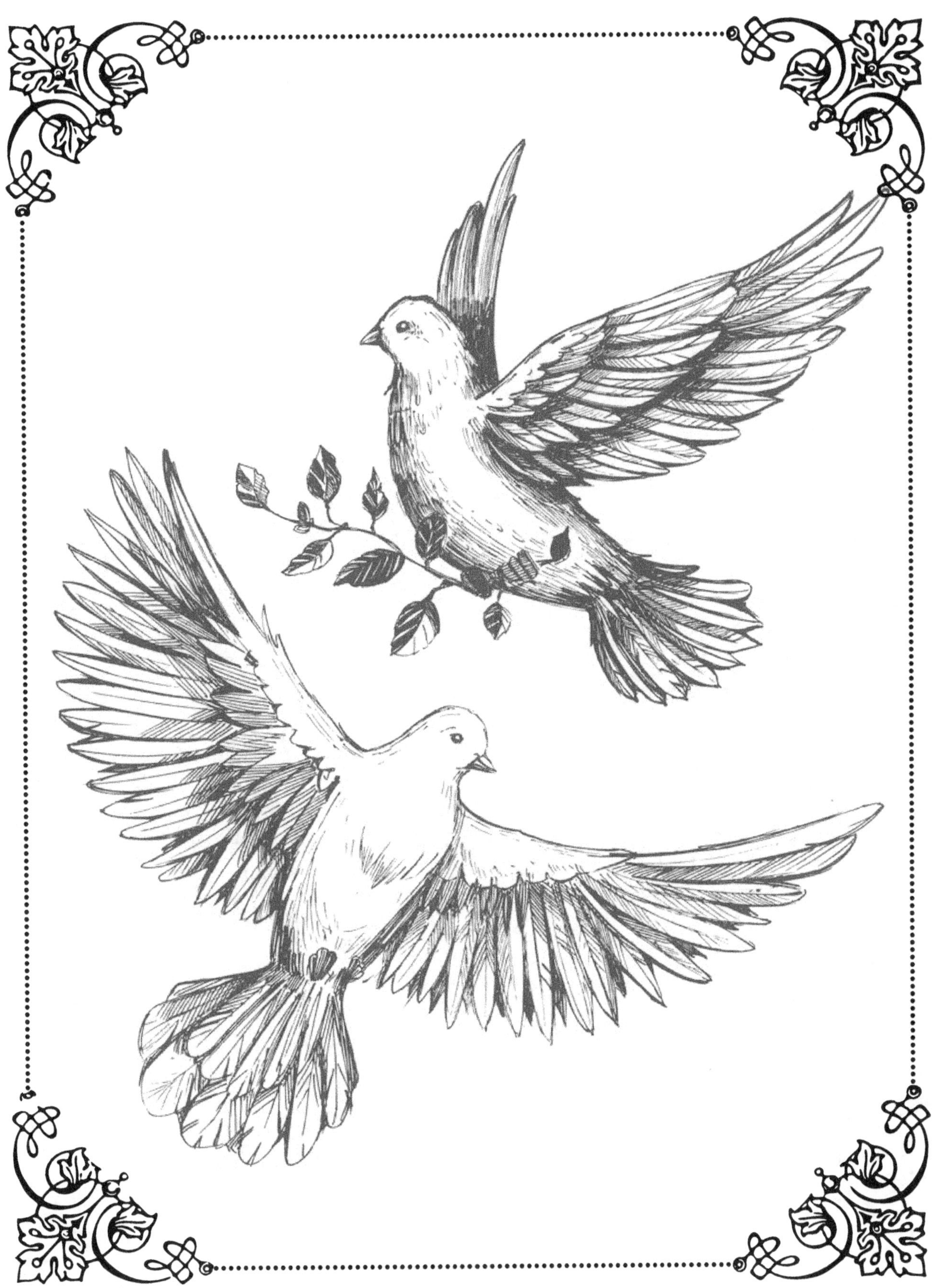

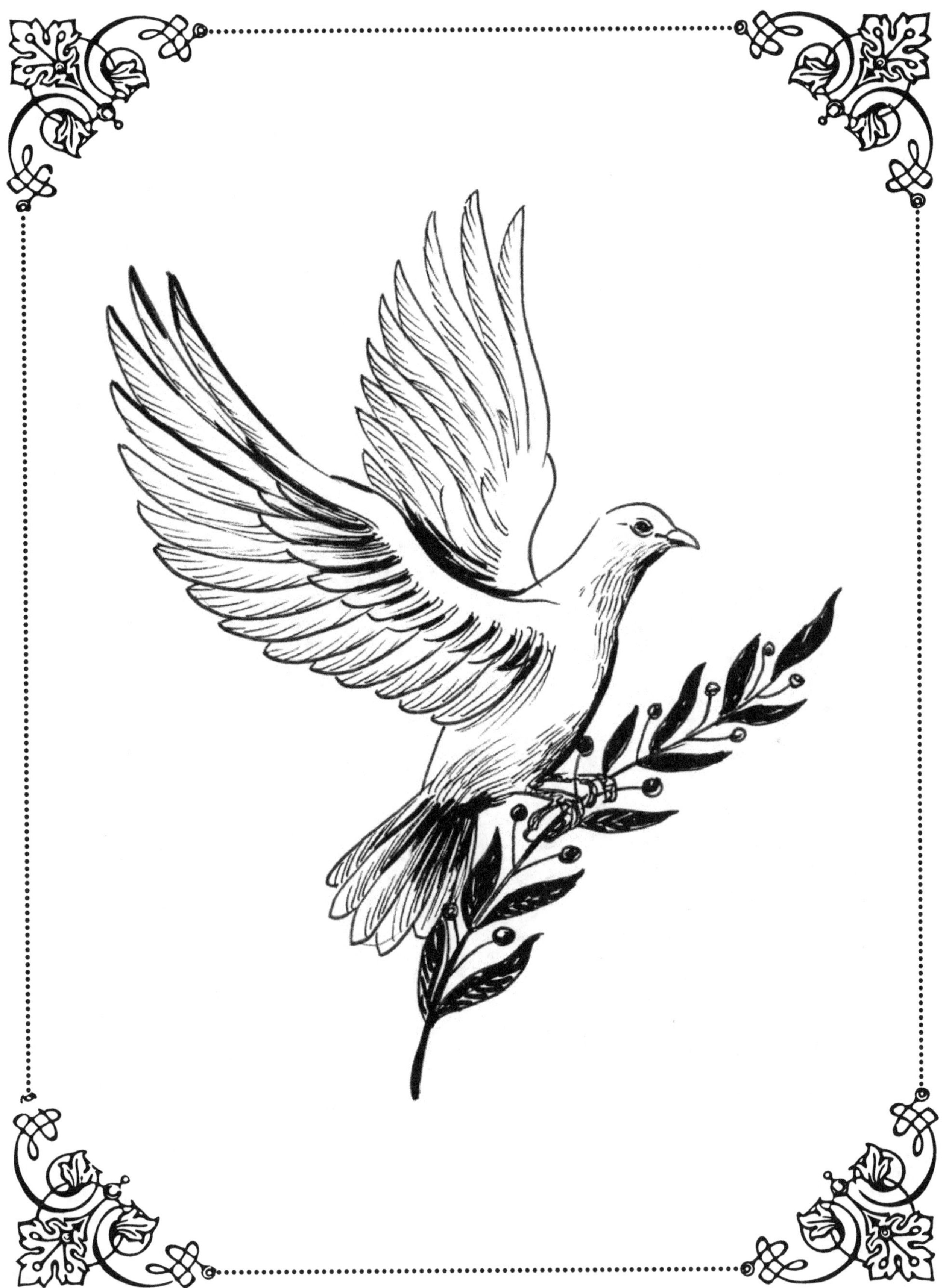

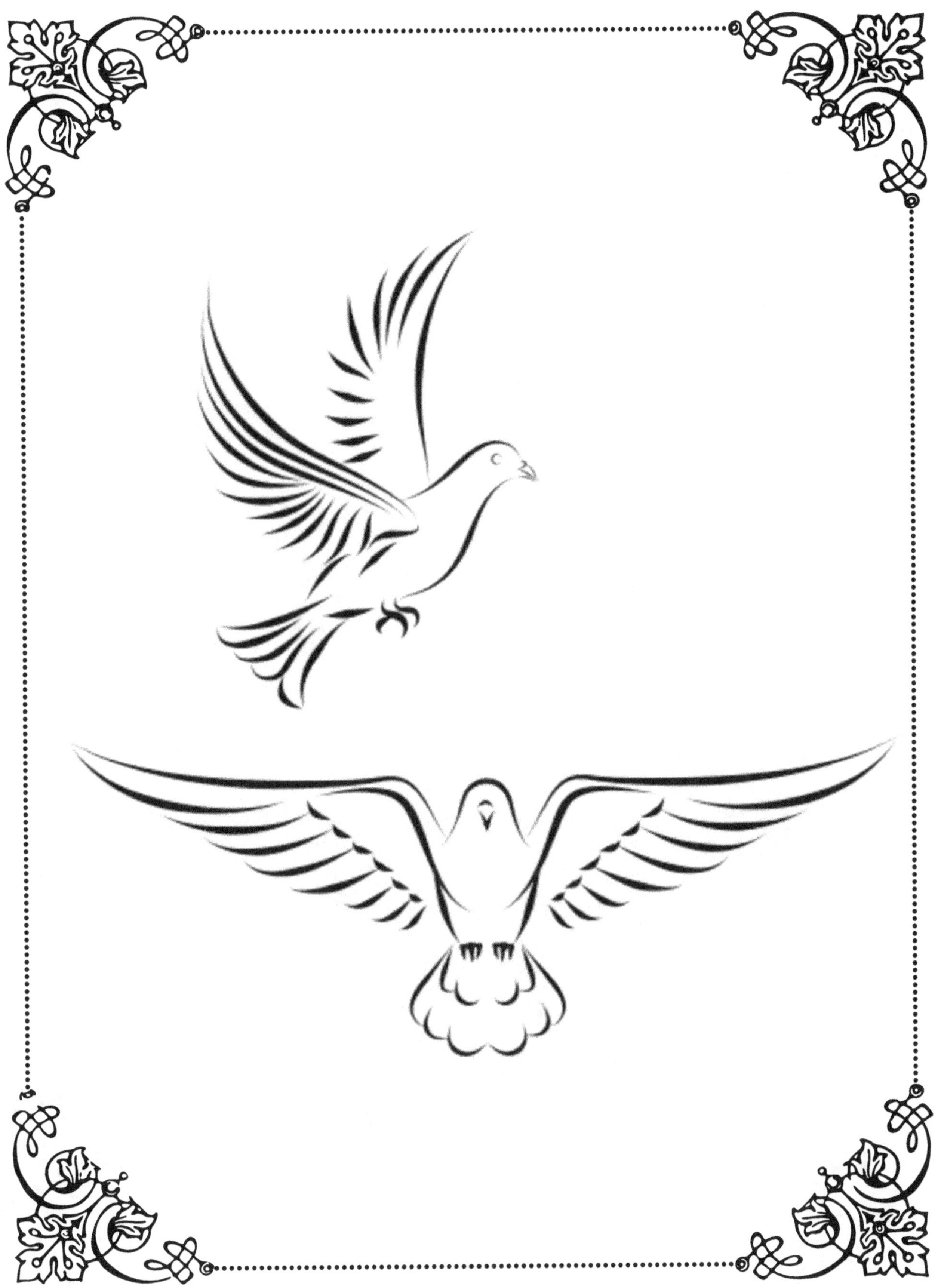

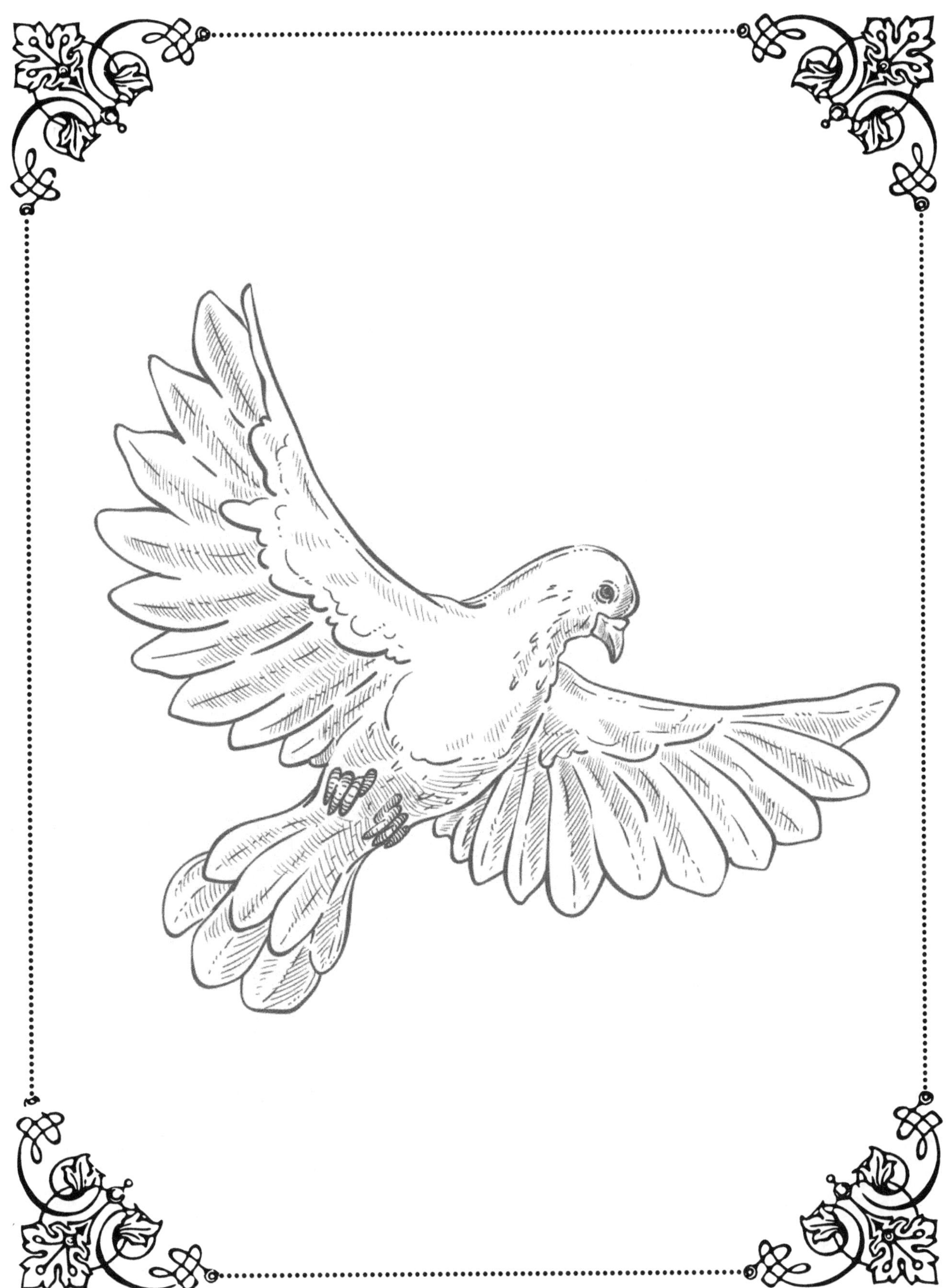

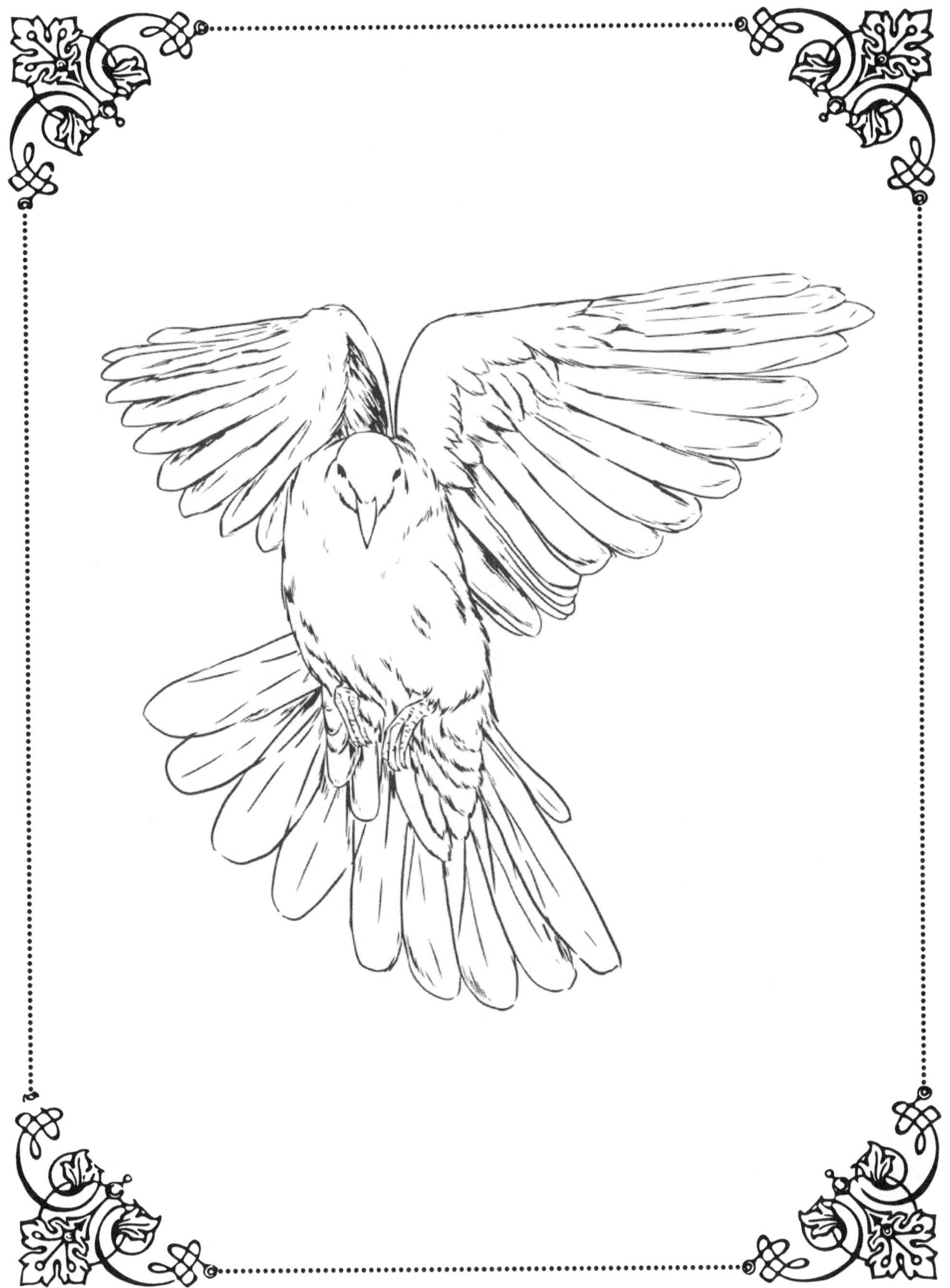

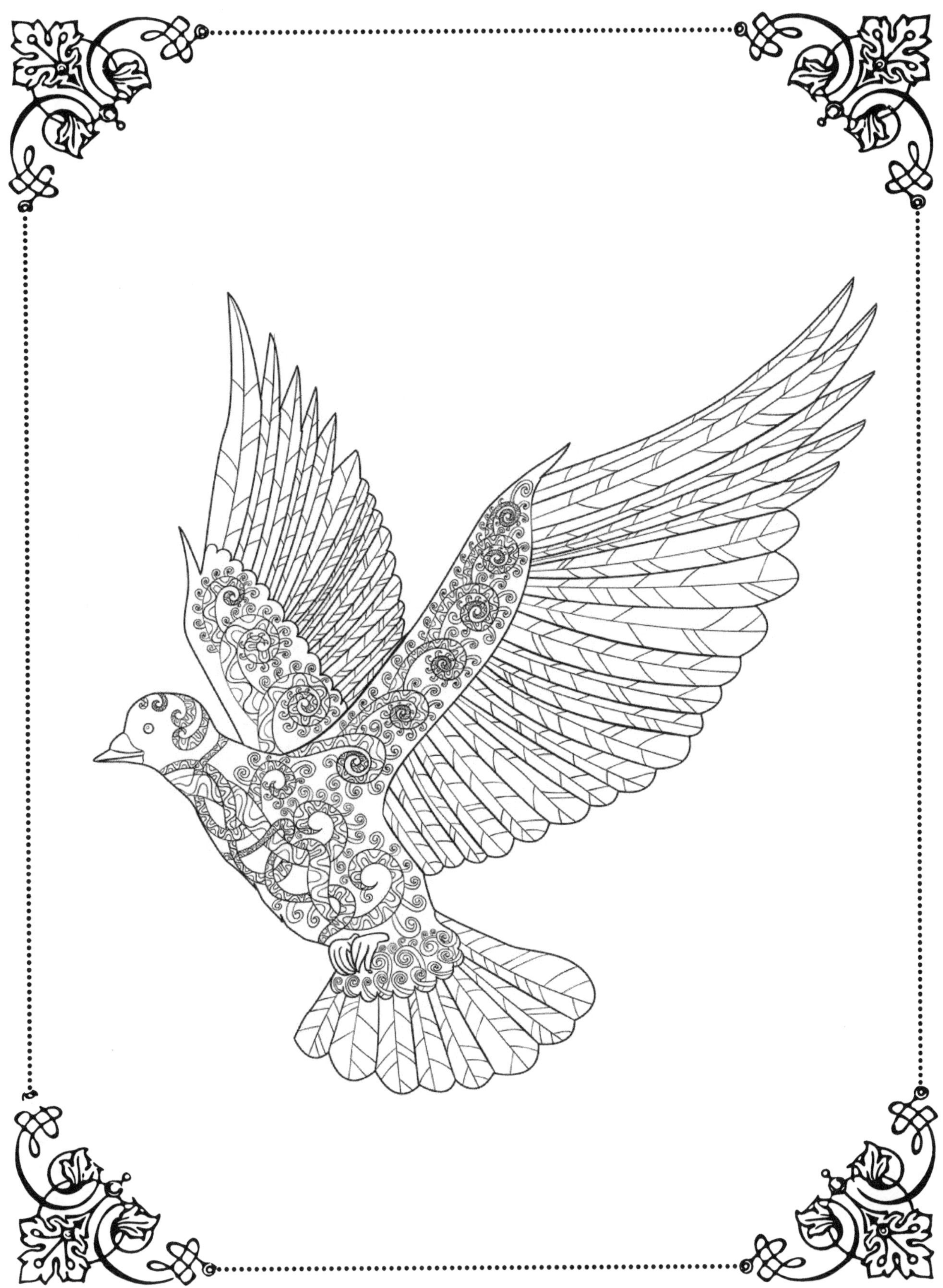

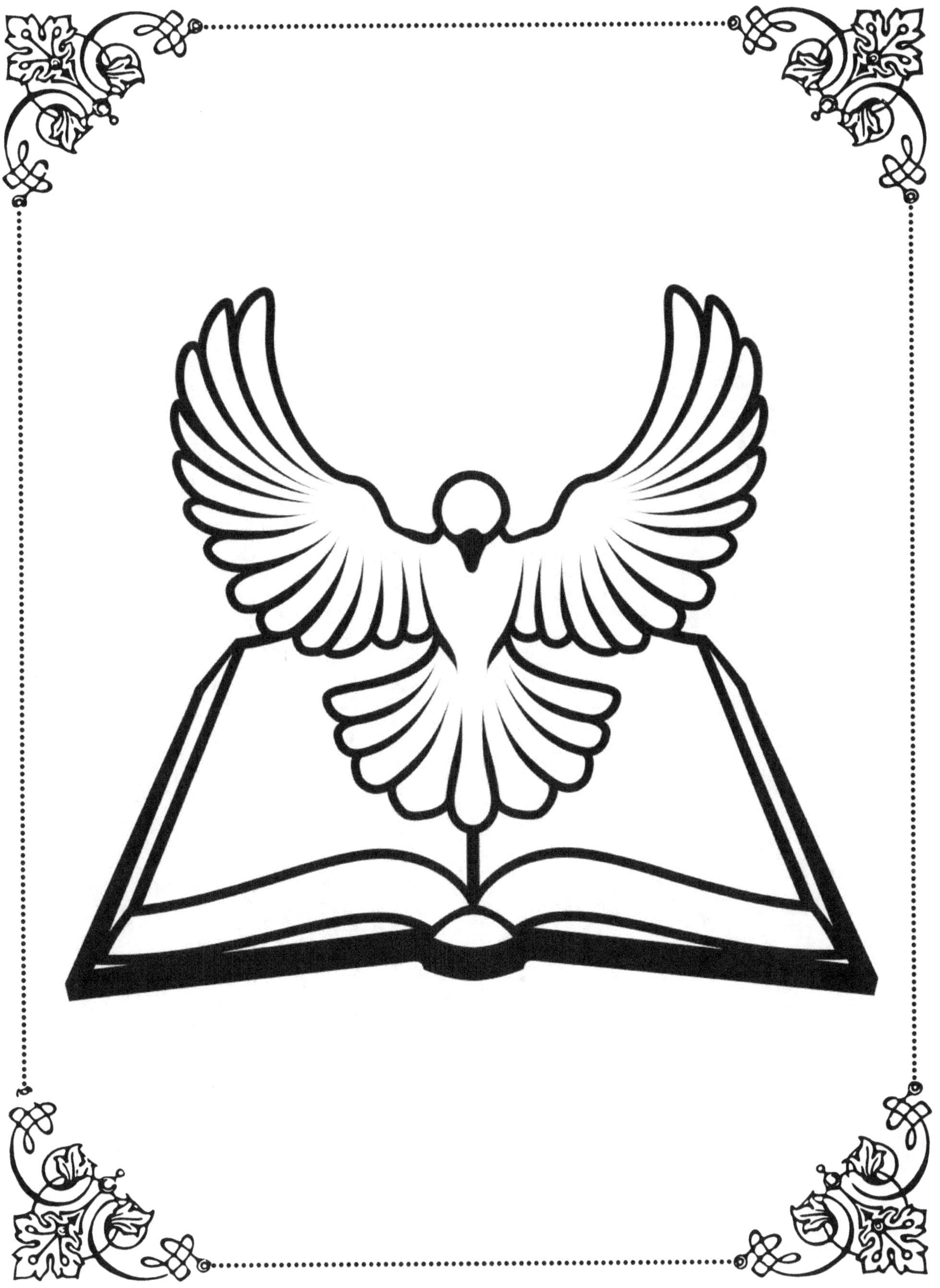

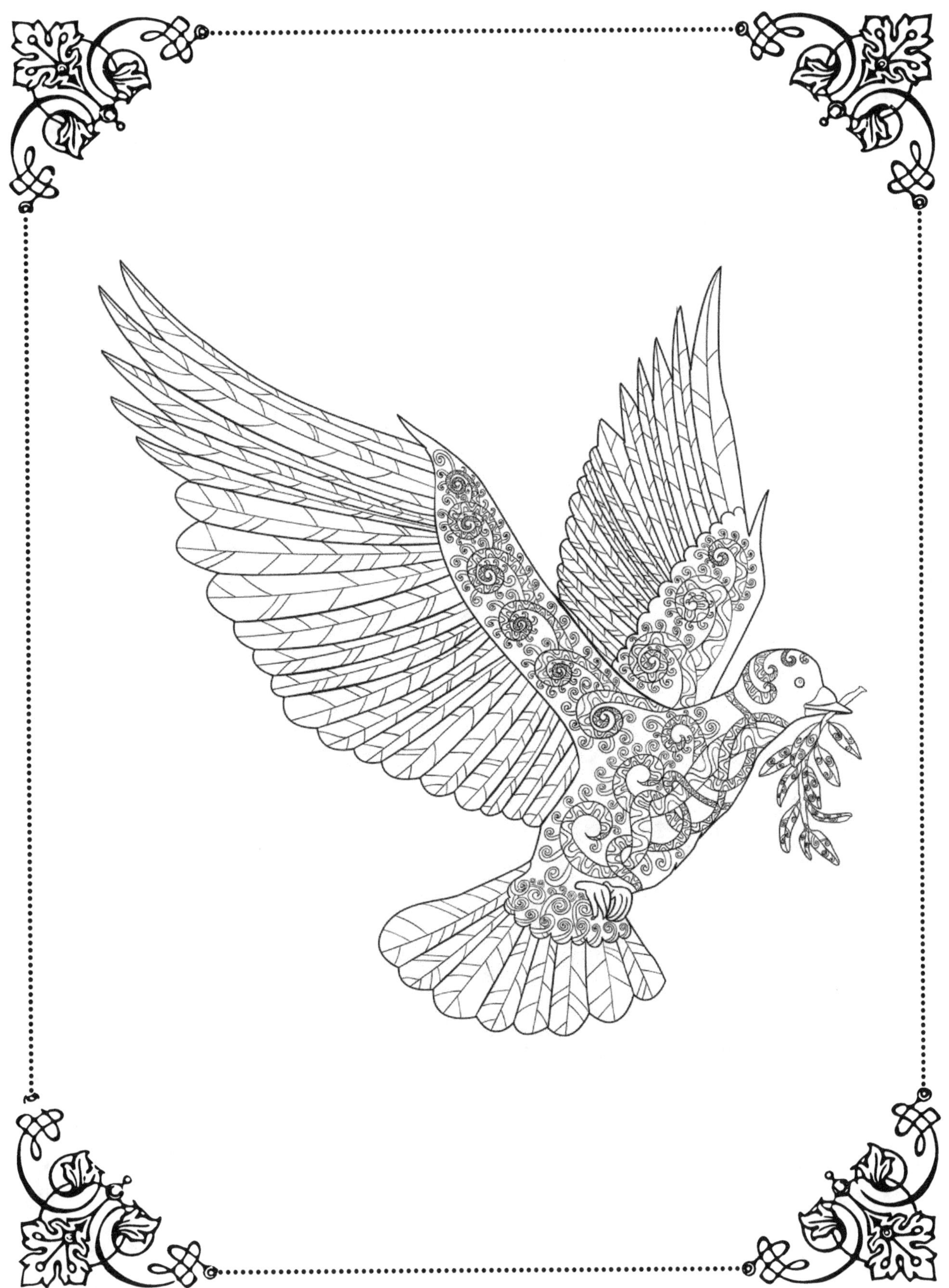

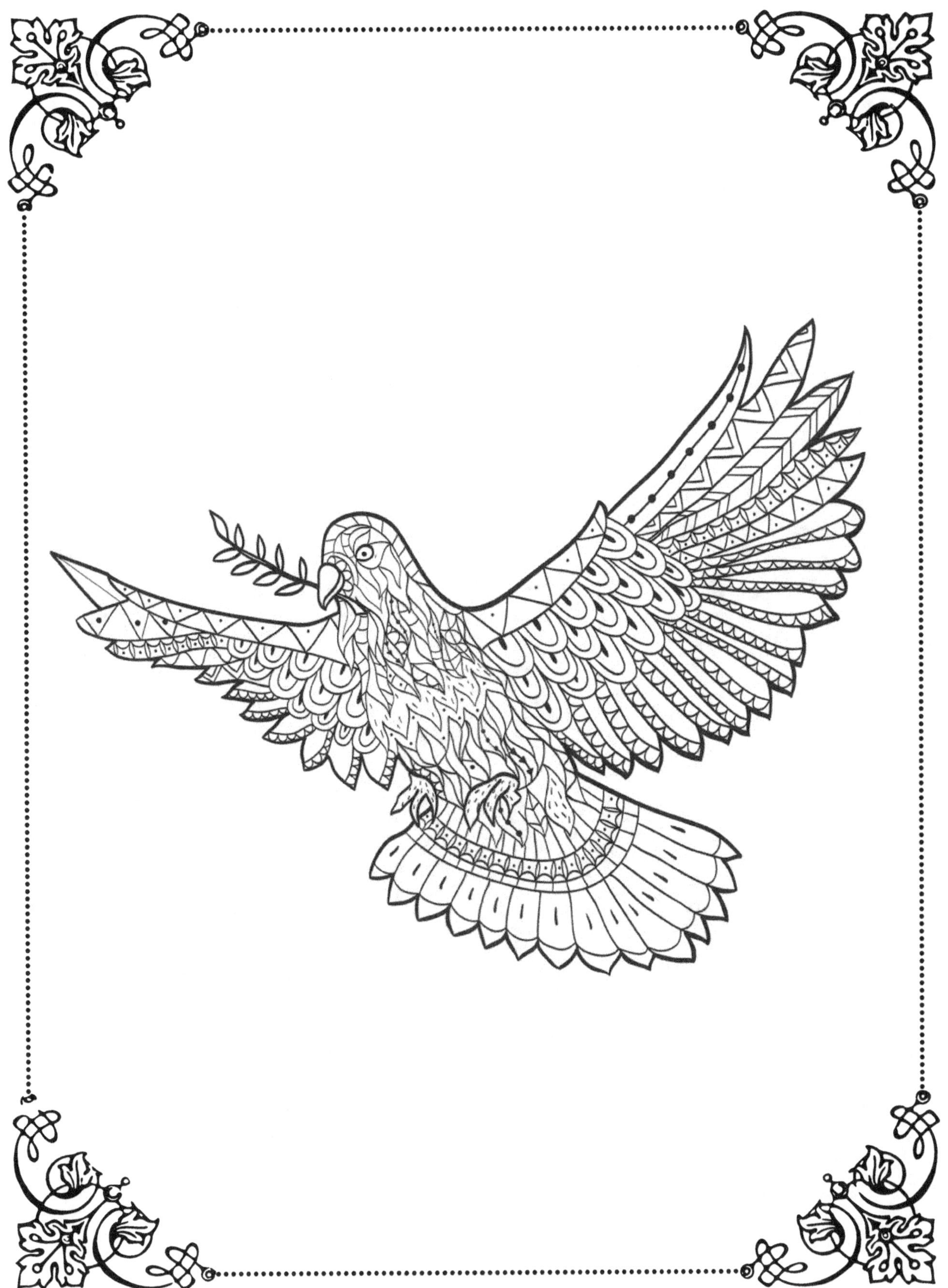

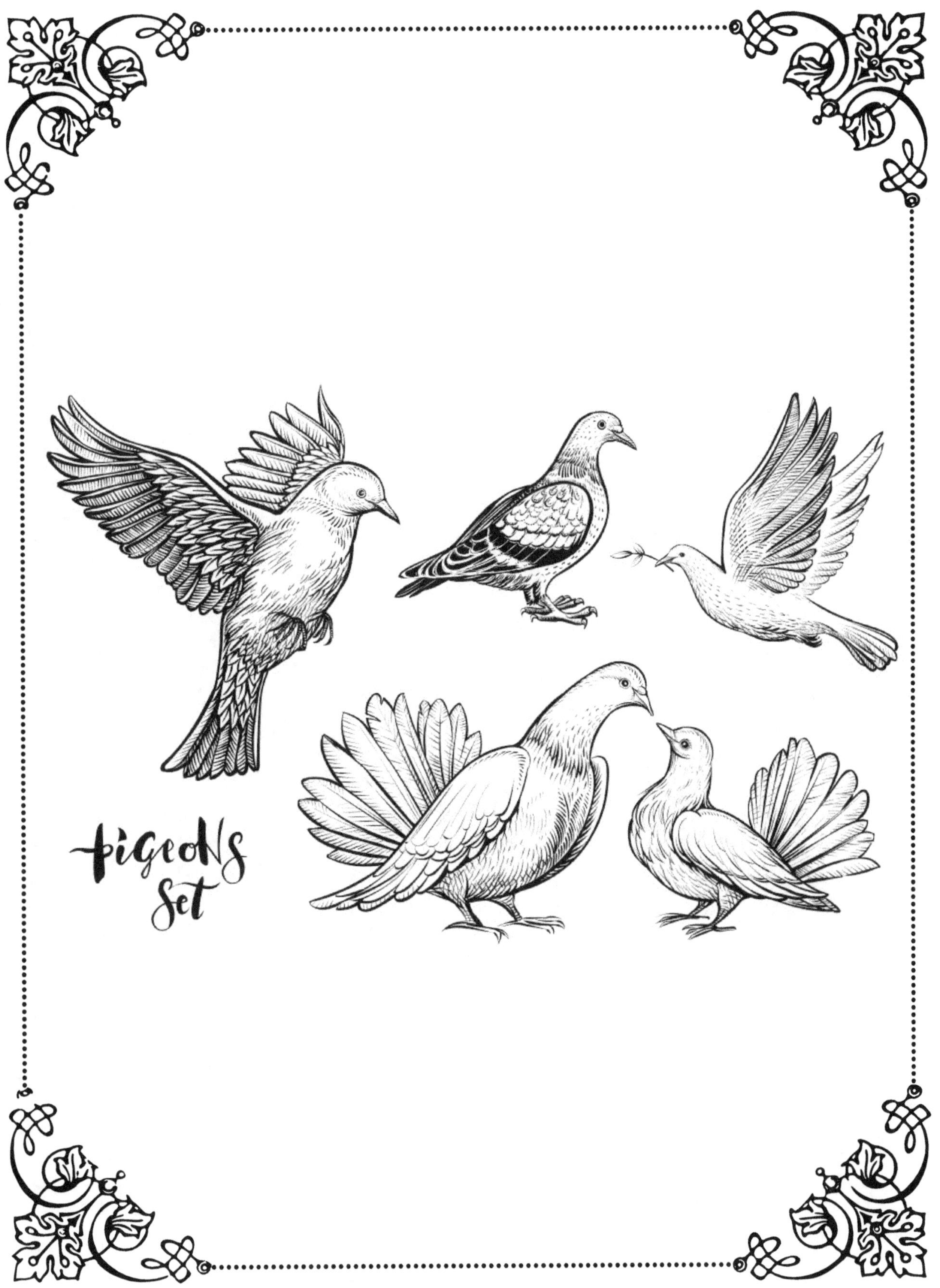
pigeons
set

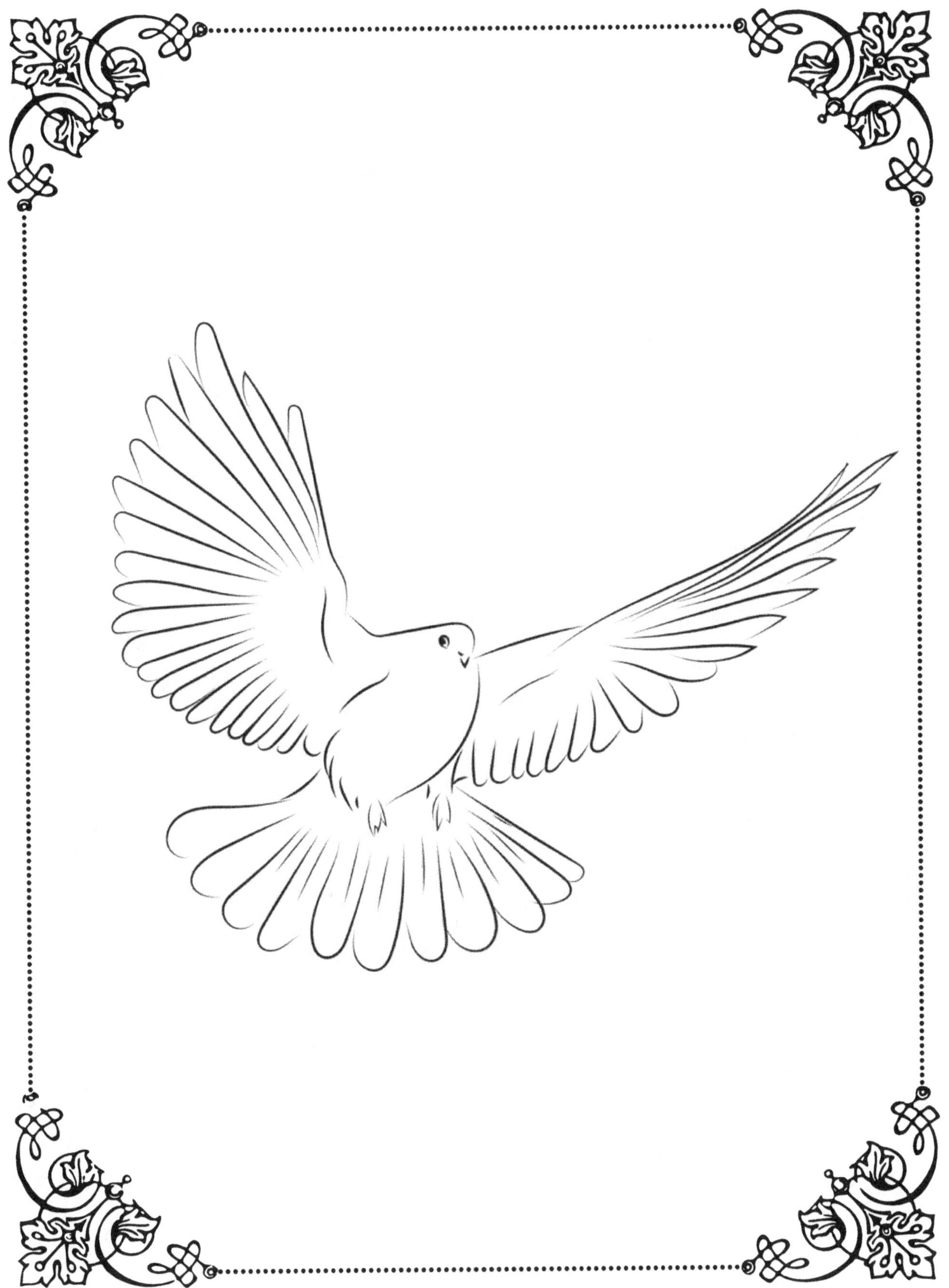

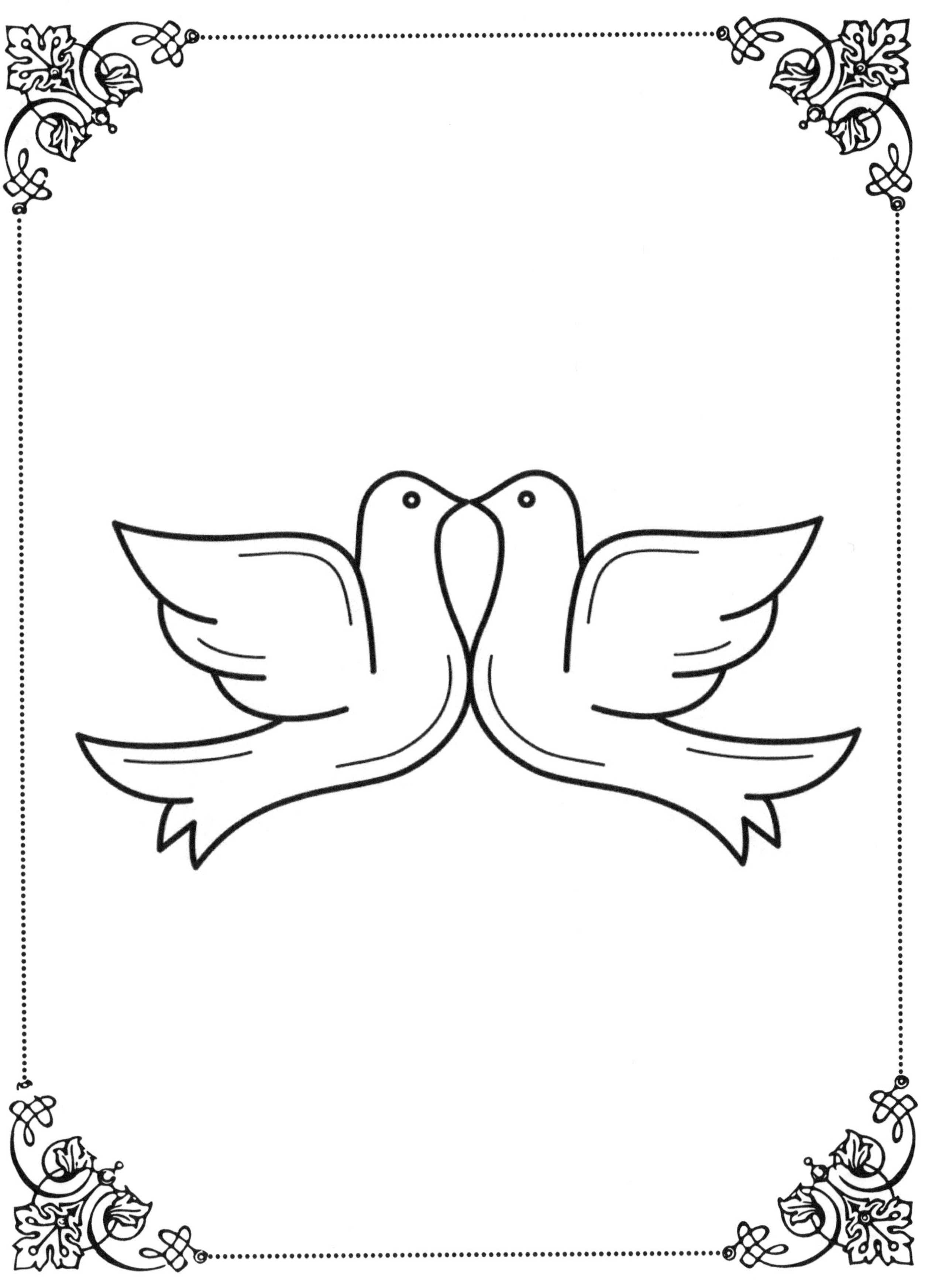

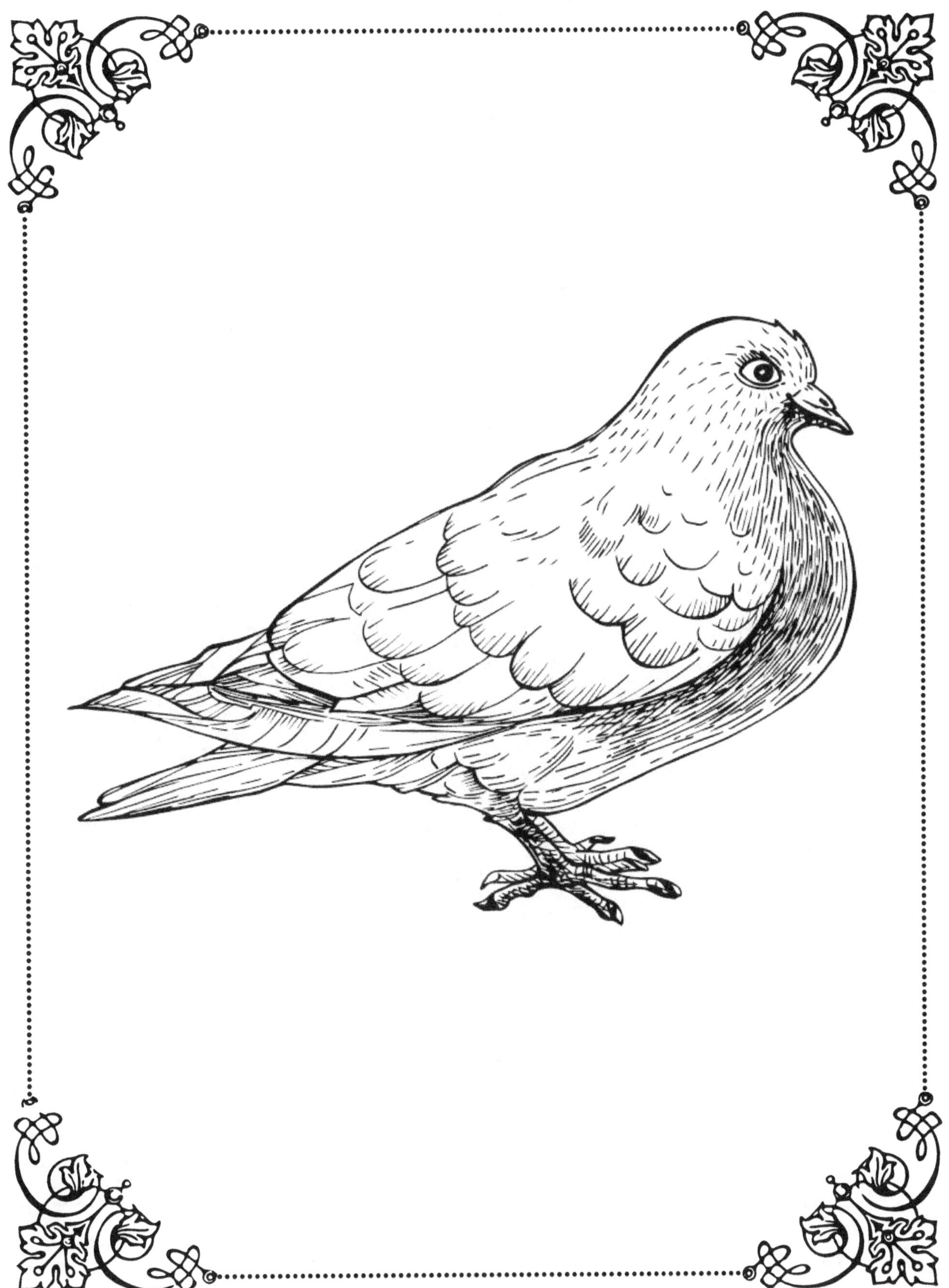

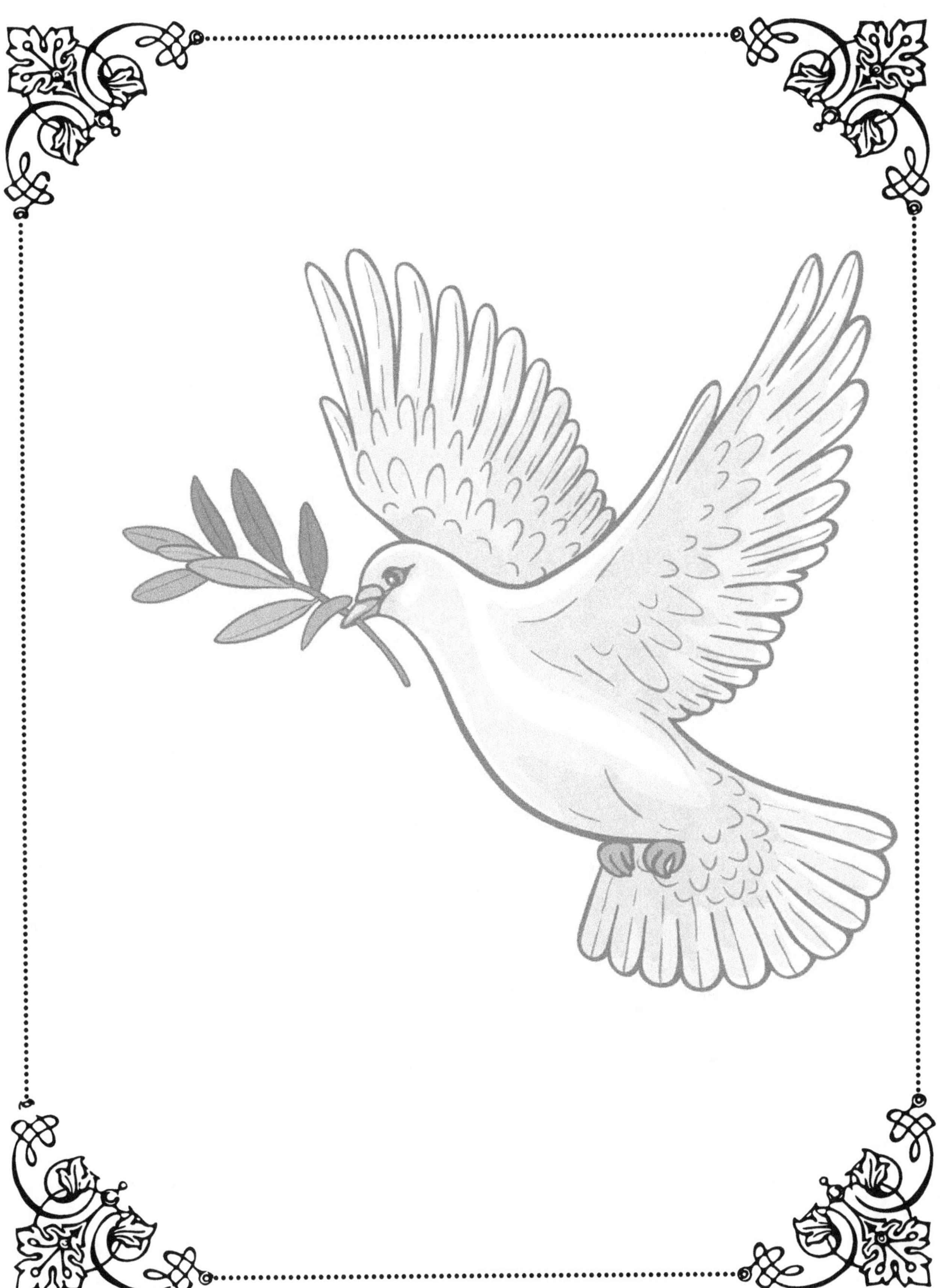

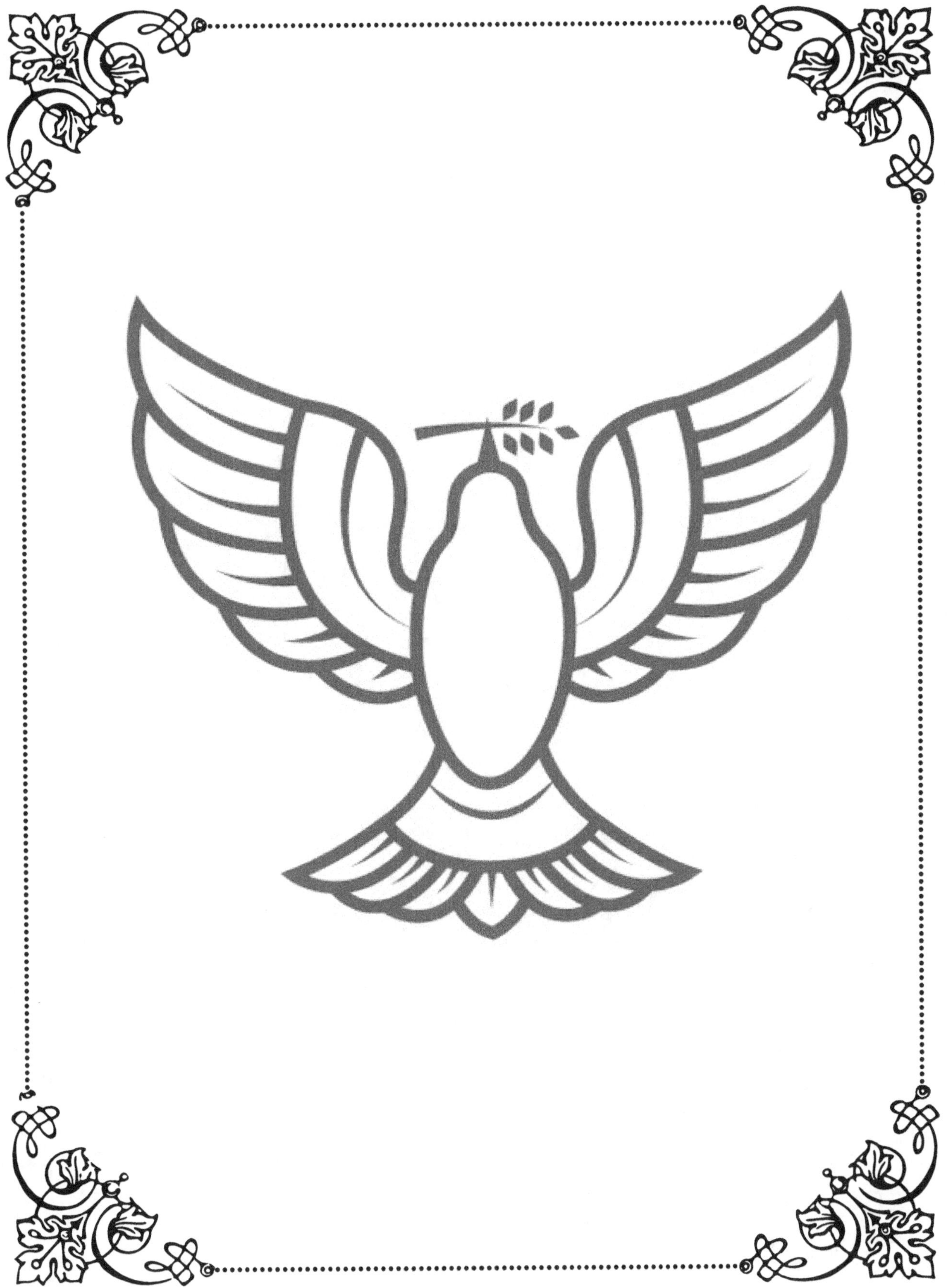

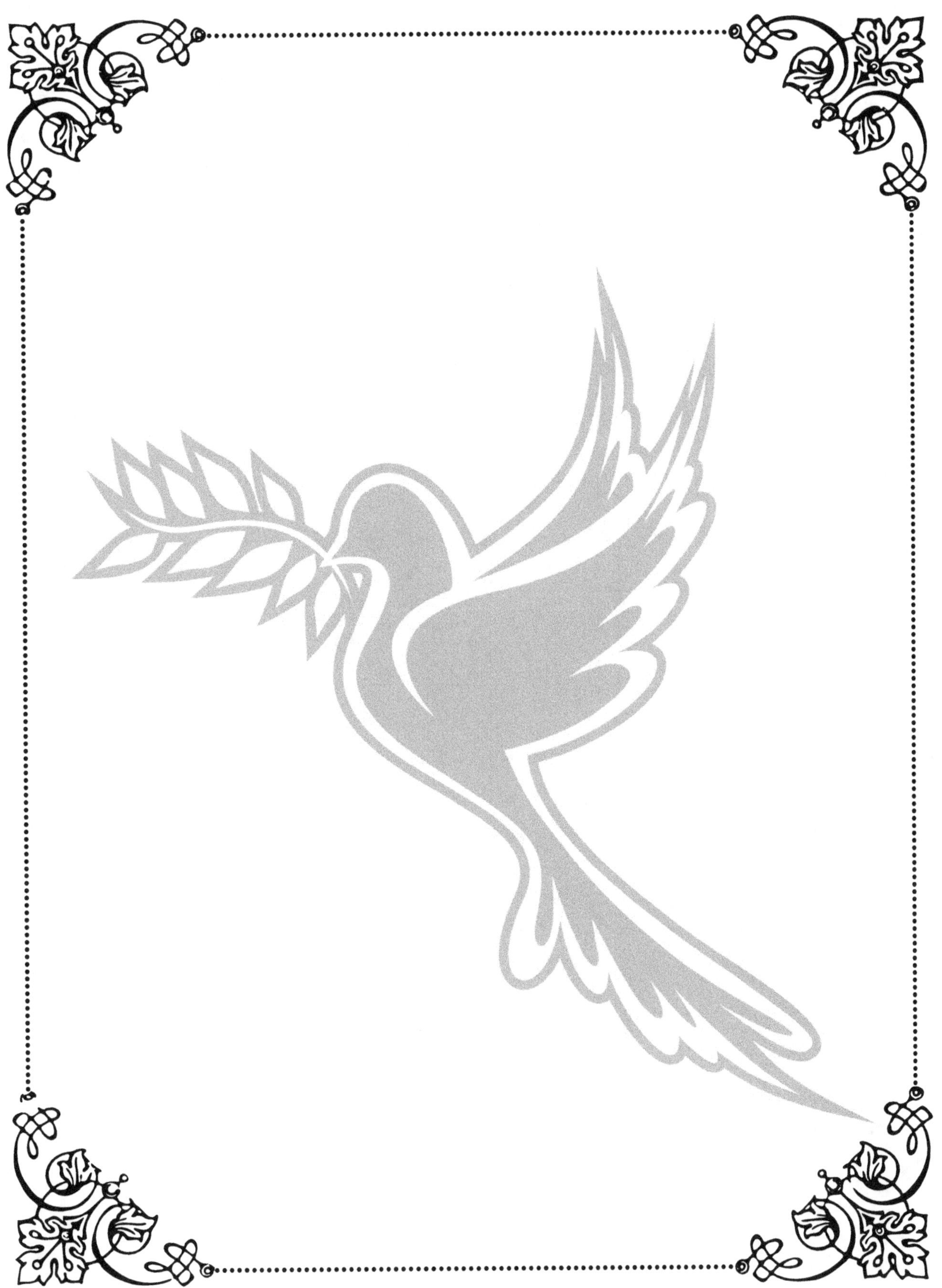

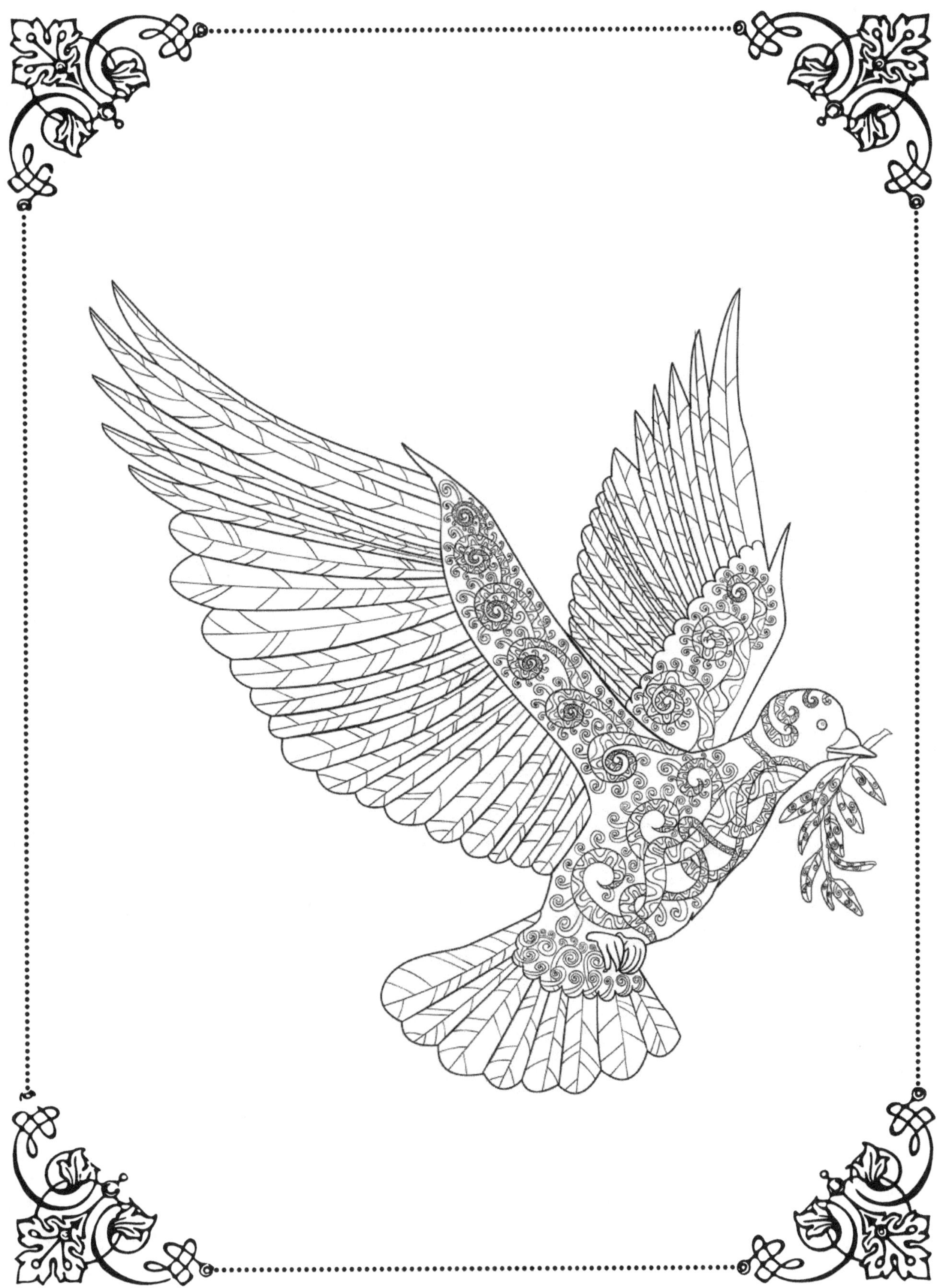

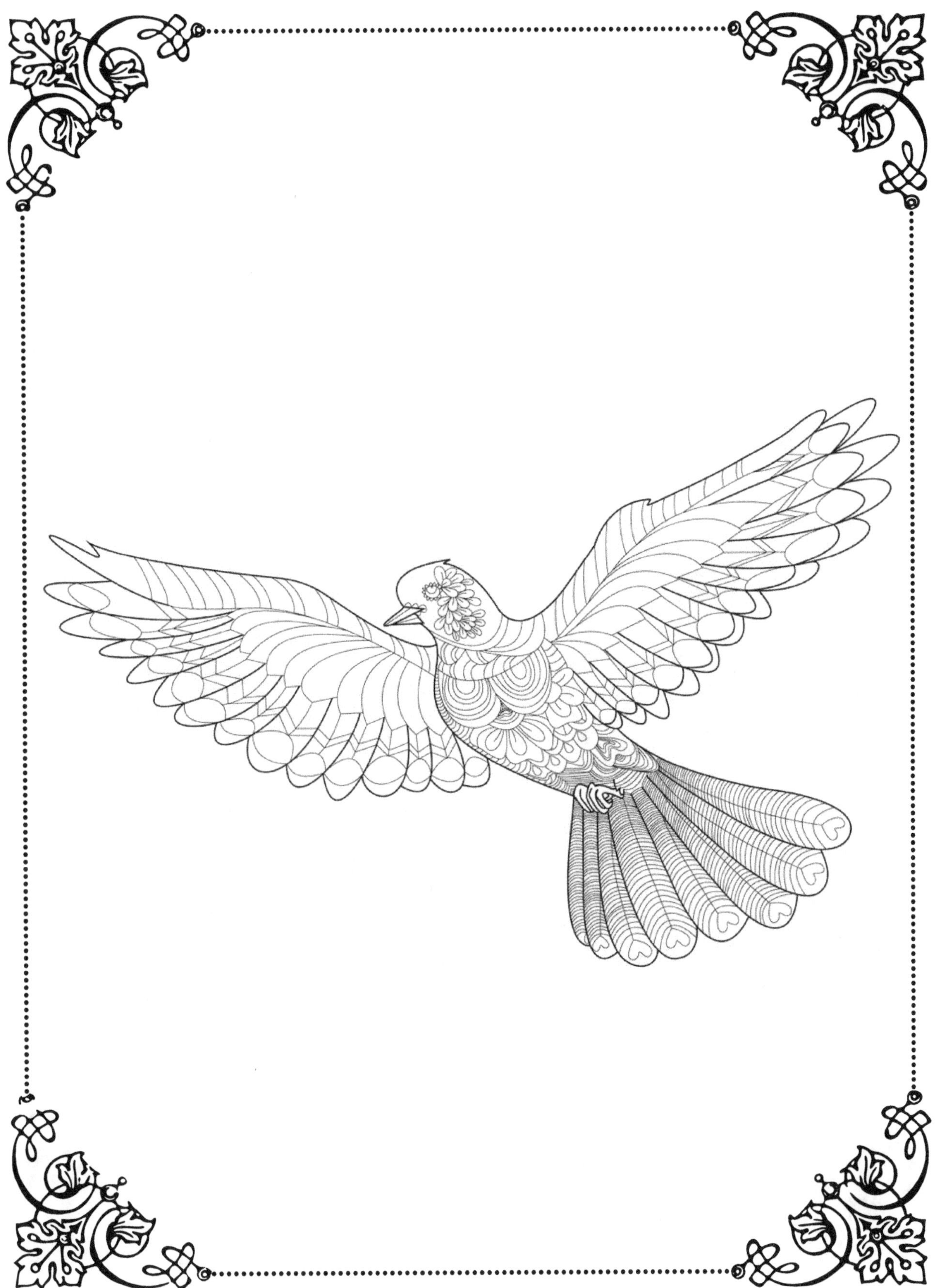